P9-CRM-189

Eyewitness
ENDANGERED ANIMALS

Golden lion
tamarin with baby

Shark fin soup

Temple viper
specimen

Mounted stag
deer head

Koala

Chainsaw used
for coppicing

Normal peregrine
falcon egg

DDT-poisoned
peregrine falcon egg

Tags used to track sharks

Warning sign
to protect
tortoises

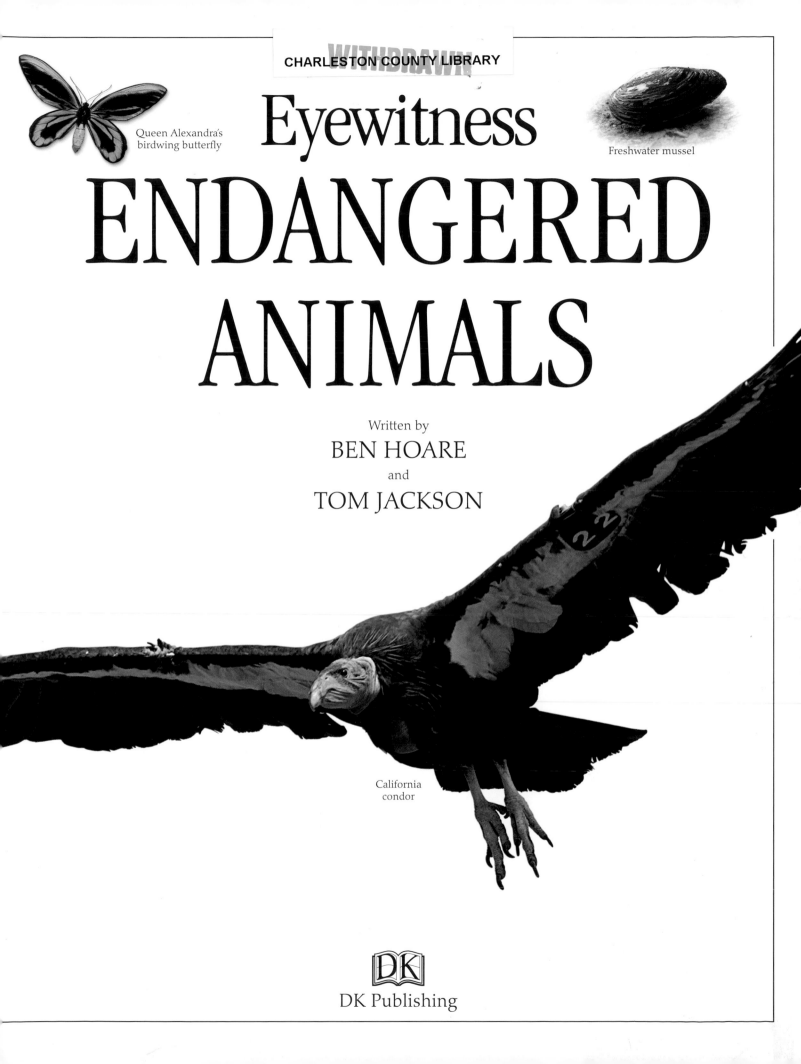

Queen Alexandra's
birdwing butterfly

Freshwater mussel

Eyewitness
ENDANGERED
ANIMALS

Written by
BEN HOARE
and
TOM JACKSON

California
condor

DK

DK Publishing

 Penguin
Random
House

Consultant Dr. Brian Groombridge

DK DELHI

Senior editor Ankush Saikia
Designer Govind Mittal
DTP designers Dheeraj Arora,
Tarun Sharma, Jagtar Singh, Preetam Singh
Editorial manager Suchismita Banerjee
Design manager Romi Chakraborty
Production manager Pankaj Sharma
Head of publishing Aparna Sharma

DK LONDON

Senior editor Dr. Rob Houston
Editor Jessamy Wood
Managing editor Julie Ferris
Managing art editor Owen Peyton Jones
Associate publisher Andrew Macintyre
Picture researcher Sarah Hopper
US editor Margaret Parrish
Production editor Siu Yin Chan
Production controller Charlotte Oliver
Jacket designer Martin Wilson

First published in the United States in 2010
by DK Publishing
345 Hudson Street, New York, New York 10014

Copyright © 2010 Dorling Kindersley Limited, London
16 10 9 8 7 6
013-175394-Sept/2010

A catalog record for this book is available from
the Library of Congress.

ISBN: 978-0-7566-6883-9 (Hardcover)
978-0-7566-6884-6 (Library binding)

Color reproduction by MDP, UK
Printed and bound in China

www.dk.com

Red-eyed tree frog

Pastrami sandwich

California quarter showing a
condor in Yosemite National Park

Fishing
reel

Shark hook

Rhinoceros
hornbill

Tray of weevil
specimens

Clown fish

Fishing rod

Contents

Gray squirrel

Wildlife under threat

LIFE IN THE WILD HAS many dangers for animals. They are always at risk of sudden attacks by predators—other animals that hunt them—and they must work hard to find enough food to survive. However, human beings make it tougher still. Humans change the world to suit themselves, clearing natural habitats, where animals live, to build cities, roads, and farms. The animals have nowhere to live and may be poisoned by the garbage humans throw away. As a result, many animal species have become endangered. Their populations are declining and they are getting rarer. If we do not help them, these species will die out and become extinct—and an extinct species is gone, forever.

PLUMMETING NUMBERS
The saiga is an unusual antelope that lives in central Asia. Its oversized nose warms up the air it breathes in winter and filters out dust in summer. It is endangered and could soon be extinct. Much of the saiga's grassland habitat has become farmland and hunters kill it for its spiral horns, which are used in Chinese medicine. Just 90 years ago there were 2 million saiga, but today only 50,000 survive.

TOO MUCH, TOO FAST
The bluefin tuna fish is a floating goldmine for fishermen. An adult fish can weigh up to 1,800 lbs (815 kg)—enough to make 25,000 pieces of sushi. But overfishing each year means there are fewer and fewer tuna to produce young fish. In just 40 years, the number of bluefin in the Atlantic Ocean has gone down by 80 percent. Attempts are being made to ban bluefin tuna fishing.

CHANGING LAND USE
The greatest danger wild animals face is from humans destroying their natural habitats. Most animals live in just one type of habitat, and if that is turned into farmland or a factory site, the animals have nowhere to go. Over the centuries, people have cleared most forests in Europe, southeastern North America, and China. Two-thirds of today's farmland was once forest full of wildlife. Habitat destruction continues at a great pace. This Amazon rain forest patch is now ringed by soybean fields.

GONE BUT NOT FORGOTTEN
The expression "as dead as a dodo" is used for something that has disappeared forever. A flightless bird that made its nest on the ground, the dodo lived only on the island of Mauritius in the Indian Ocean. It was one of the first animals known to have been made extinct by people. The slow-moving dodo was easy to hunt, and its numbers began declining when people started to settle on Mauritius in the 17th century. In less than 50 years, the dodos were all wiped out.

STAR ANIMALS

These tourists are on a tiger safari in Ranthambore National Park in northern India. Threatened species such as the tiger have become powerful symbols of conservation. Every time we see a tiger we are reminded that it is in danger and that it needs to be protected. Tourists who pay to visit protected conservation areas such as national parks contribute to their maintenance.

NO ONE IS SAFE

Rare animals are at the most risk of extinction—it does not take much to wipe them out. However, common species may fall sharply in number and need to be protected, too. In the 1970s, the house sparrow used to be common across Europe, even in the biggest cities. It is now a much rarer sight there, possibly due to a fall in the number of insects it preyed on.

DOING THE RIGHT THING

Francis of Assisi is the Christian patron saint of animals. There are many stories about how this 12th-century monk cared for animals because he believed it was the right thing to do. Today's conservationists protect endangered animals for similar reasons. They believe that animals add to the beauty and variety of life around us and that they have as much right to exist in this world as humans do.

CONSERVATION WORKS

African white rhinoceroses were under serious threat from poachers who killed them for their horns. In some areas there were just a handful of rhinos left in the wild. Today, there are about 18,000 wild white rhinos—nearly all the southern white subspecies. The southern white rhino's numbers increased following conservation measures such as providing safe areas for the rhinos and forbidding the buying and selling of rhino horn. However, the northern white rhino is now feared to be extinct in the wild.

What is a species?

When all the members of an animal species have died, there is no turning back—that species is extinct. Before conservationists know if an animal is endangered, or in danger of becoming extinct, they must figure out the total number of members of its species, in all parts of the world. So what is a species? A species is a group of animals that look very similar to one another and live in the same manner. But there is another more important connection—an animal can breed successfully only with a member of its own species.

Soprano pipistrelle

THE SAME, BUT DIFFERENT
It is not always easy for us to tell one species from another. Until 1999, the common pipistrelle bat in Europe was thought to be one distinct species. But scientists noticed some of these bats were sopranos—they produced higher calls than others. The soprano bats only mated with each other and never with their deeper-voiced neighbors. Though similar looking, they mate in two groups, and so are two species: the common and the soprano.

Common pipistrelle

Avium is the Latin word for birds

TABULA II.

AVIUM *capita & artus.*

1. ACCIPITRIS roftrum uncinatum cum denticulo maxillæ fuperioris;
   e *Falcone.*

2. PICÆ roftrum cultratum;
   e *Corvo.*

3. ANSERIS roftrum denticulatum;
   ex *Anate.*

4. SCOLOPACIS roftrum cylindricum cum gibbo maxillæ inferioris;
   e *Numenio.*

5. GALLINÆ roftrum cum maxilla fuperior imbricata;
   e *Gallo.*

6. PASSERIS roftrum conicum;
   e *Fringilla.*

7. Pes FISSUS digitis folutis;
   e *Paffere;*

8. Pes SEMIPALMATUS;
   e *Scolopace.*

9. Pes PALMATUS;
   ex *Anfere;*

10. Pes digitis duobus anticis, totidemque po cis; e *Pico.*

11. RECTRICES *Caudæ* 1. 2. 3. 4. 5. 6. 12. 11. 10. 9. 8. 7.

12. REMIGES *Alæ* 1. 2. 3. 4. 5. 6. 9. 10. 11. 12. 13. 14. 15, 16. 17. 1

Asiatic lion

DISTANT COUSINS
The lion is one of the so-called big cats and is found mainly in Africa, but lions once lived across Europe and parts of Asia, too. Today, a tiny population of Asiatic lions survives in the Gir National Park in western India. The Asiatic lions are the same species as their African cousins, but there have been no matings between the two groups, or subspecies, for centuries. As a result, the Asiatic lion now looks different, with a smaller build and a thinner mane.

Carl Linnaeus

WHAT'S IN A NAME?
A single animal may be known by different names in different languages. To avoid confusion, every species has a two-part scientific name. For example, *Anas platyrhynchos* is the scientific name for the mallard duck. This system was devised by Swedish scientist Carl Linnaeus in the 1750s. He put each species into a group, or genus. The mallard's genus name is *Anas*, while *platyrhynchos* is its specific name—referring to the mallard species. Above is Linnaeus's book *Systema Naturae*, first published in 1735.

OUT OF THE DEEP

Some animal species have rarely been seen alive by people because they live so deep in the ocean. For instance, the colossal squid was first described in 1925 when two of its giant tentacles were found in a sperm whale's stomach. In 2007, this colossal squid was the first adult of its species ever to be caught. The species had evaded capture by humans, despite growing up to 40 ft (12 m) long.

Animals were grouped according to similarities, such as the shape of birds' feet

REVERT TO TYPE

Even animal experts get puzzled sometimes when identifying animals. They must then refer to the description of the species made by the person who discovered it. This description consists of drawings and often a preserved "type specimen." This jar contains a specimen of a temple viper, a dangerous tree snake from Southeast Asia. The formaldehyde liquid in the jar stops the snake's body from decaying, so it has stayed preserved for decades.

Astraptes fulgerator (variation 1)

Astraptes fulgerator (variation 2)

ALL IN THE GENES

A recent way of distinguishing a new species is genetic barcoding. This technology compares a short strand of DNA (the material containing an animal's genes) from one animal with that of another. Scientists do not need all the genes, or DNA sequences, to figure out if animals belong to different species. DNA barcoding told scientists that these look-alike blue skipper butterflies from the genus *Astraptes* could actually be two distinct species. One day, portable DNA scanners might be able to identify any animal, anywhere.

Green skin turns brown in shade

DO I KNOW YOU?

Members of a species normally look similar to one another. They identify each other by how they look, and biologists do the same. For example, this lizard is a green anole. It moves a flap of pink skin on its throat to attract other members of its species. A closely related species, the brown anole, does the same, except its throat flap is orange.

Eye sees in color

Throat flap is pushed in and out

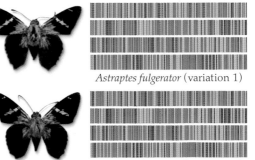

Adapting and survival

EVERY SPECIES HAS ITS OWN special way of life. Giraffes and warthogs both live on African grasslands, but the two species have adapted to this habitat in different ways. Giraffes stretch their long necks to reach treetop leaves, while warthogs kneel to graze on grass. In 1859, English naturalist Charles Darwin described how life on Earth evolved to be so different. The process is driven by "the survival of the fittest."

The fittest animals are those best suited to their particular way of life. A fit giraffe has a longer neck and can get more food than giraffes with shorter necks. The fittest animals survive and have offspring, while the weaker ones die out. Darwin called this natural selection— nature determines which animals thrive. Habitats change, and new animals become a success. Slowly, the animals evolve into other species. But when a habitat is damaged quickly by human activity, even the fittest animals struggle to survive.

EXTREME EVOLUTION
Every species evolves within what biologists call a niche. A niche describes where the animal lives, the food it eats, and how it mates and avoids danger. Some animals have evolved bizarre adaptations in their niches, such as the aye-aye found only on the island of Madagascar. In the absence of woodpeckers on the island, the aye-aye fills their niche. It feeds on insect grubs hidden under tree bark. The aye-aye taps tree branches and trunks listening out for hollows made by grubs. Then it bites a hole through the bark and pokes in its elongated middle finger to pick out the grub, just like a woodpecker would do with its beak and tongue.

TREE OF LIFE
Darwin's great discovery was seeing how new species could evolve from other species. He said that species that look similar, such as horses and zebras, must have evolved from the same ancestor. Darwin made this tree sketch in 1837 to show how evolving species branched off from each other as they adapted in different ways in different habitats.

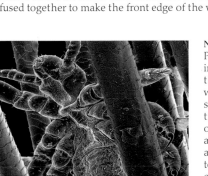

Long-eared bat

Thumb claw points from the front of the wing

Feathers make wings larger, lighter, and more flexible

Red-crowned crane

EVOLVING TWICE

Evolution consists of the tiny changes in the genetic material (DNA) of a species from one generation to the next. The accumulated differences can over time result in the emergence of a new species. Evolution sometimes comes up with the same answers many times over. For example, bats and birds can both fly, but they evolved wings in different ways. Birds evolved from feathered dinosaurs, while bats are flying mammals that evolved after the dinosaurs had died out. The scientific name for bats is *Chiroptera*, or "hand wings," because their wings are made from skin stretched out between long finger bones. The same hand bones are inside a bird's feathered wing, only they are fused together to make the front edge of the wing.

WARNING FROM HISTORY

In the 19th century, English naturalist Alfred Russell Wallace studied the animals of Malaysia and Indonesia. Wallace came up with the same ideas about evolution as his friend Darwin. While in Southeast Asia, Wallace also saw rain forests being cleared to make way for tea plantations. He realized that species were being endangered when their habitats were destroyed.

NO PLACE LIKE HOME

Parasites are animals that live on (or even inside) other animals, which are known as the hosts. Most parasites evolve together with a single host species and cannot survive on any other. Human head lice are tiny bloodsuckers that live under the hair of the head. They cannot survive for long away from people, even on other hairy animals—they must drink human blood to live. When an animal species becomes extinct, its dedicated parasites die out, too.

Large ears pick up calls from other koalas

GENERALISTS AND SPECIALISTS

Animals such as rats, mice, and raccoons are generalists. Generalists eat all types of food and can find it pretty much anywhere. They first evolved in wild places, but often do just as well living in artificial habitats, such as cities. Specialist animals are just the opposite. The koala, which lives only in Australia, eats only leaves from certain eucalyptus trees. It cannot survive without this particular food. Specialist animals are often the most endangered.

Long, curved beak used for digging out insects

DARWIN'S INSPIRATION

Charles Darwin got many of his ideas for the theory of natural selection by studying the animals of the Galápagos Islands in the eastern Pacific Ocean. Many of them are endangered today, including this Floreana mockingbird. Darwin noticed that the mockingbirds on each island had slight differences. Some had paler feathers, others had longer, hooked beaks. He realized that these differences helped the birds survive in the particular conditions of their own islands.

The variety of life

No one knows exactly how many types of animal there are. So far, scientists have made a list of 1.5 million species, but many think the total number could be nearer to 30 million. This great diversity of life—or biodiversity—came about through evolution over billions of years. Animals now survive almost everywhere on Earth, from the depths of the ocean floor to the hot desert sands. Such great variety makes the natural world fragile, since it is all too easy for unusual animals to become endangered. At the same time, biodiversity makes wildlife resilient. Evolution thrives on variation, and so animal life will always be able to adapt to whatever nature throws at it.

CROWDED FORESTS
Tropical rain forests are the most crowded places on Earth. Two-thirds of all animal species live in rain forests. There are many places to survive in such a habitat—from the very top of a tree to the undergrowth on the forest floor. When the daytime animals retire in the evening, a whole new set appears during the night. Jungle researchers are always finding new species, mainly types of insect. They beat tree branches and collect the little animals that fall out. A single tree can sometimes contain hundreds of species.

AN ANIMAL KINGDOM
These colorful corals may look like sea plants but they are really tiny relatives of jellyfish. Millions of corals live together in enormous colonies held together by their branching skeletons made from calcium carbonate. As each layer of corals dies, a new one grows on top of the chalky skeletons left behind. Over time, corals form intricate reef systems that provide shelter to many types of fish, shrimp, octopus, and sea snake. The diversity of life found in these reefs makes them comparable to rain forests.

Reef fish look for food among corals

Corals grow in many shapes, including plant-like branches

ZONES OF LIFE

The huge wealth of habitats across Earth's surface is created by different climates and landforms. The freezing poles are covered in ice or tundra, while steamy forests grow in the rain-drenched tropics. This map divides Earth into 11 regions known as biomes. Each biome is home to a particular set of animals that is adapted to the challenges of life there.

- Grassland
- Desert
- Tropical forest
- Temperate forest
- Coniferous forest
- Tundra
- Mountains
- Ice cap
- Lakes, rivers, and wetlands
- Open ocean
- Coral reef
- Urban area

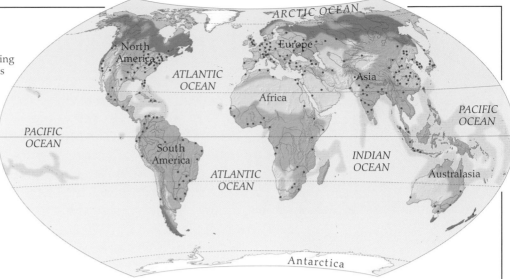

STRENGTH IN NUMBERS

The largest animals in the world are mammals, but Earth is not ruled by the likes of elephants, bears, and whales. Instead, Earth is overrun by insects and other small, hard-to-spot species. There are at least 200 insect species for every mammal species, maybe even more. When it comes to diversity, mammal species are at the bottom—even bird, reptile, and fish species easily outnumber them.

Birds 9,990 species

Mammals 5,488 species

Reptiles 8,734 species

Insects 950,000 species

Fish 30,700 species

A VERY HOT HOME

Animals cling to life in some very unusual places. These crabs and shellfish live on a volcano deep under the ocean. Scientists discovered these communities only in the 1970s. There are no seaweeds or other plants to eat down there. Instead, the animals feed on bacteria. The bacteria get their energy from chemicals pumped into the water by boiling hot volcanic springs. This is one of the few places on Earth where life exists without the Sun's energy.

Label identifies the species

ANIMAL LIBRARIES

Taxonomy is the science of identifying species. Taxonomists work in museums, studying animals collected from around the world. They are always looking for new species and try to work out how an animal might be related to other species. This tray of weevil specimens is from the Natural History Museum in London, England. The museum has the largest collection of animals on Earth. Its millions of specimens fill cabinets and shelves that, when laid out in a line, would stretch to 2 miles (3 km). However, taxonomists will never be able to list all the species present on Earth, and many animals become extinct before they can even be identified.

Links in the chain

ANIMALS DO NOT LIVE IN ISOLATION. Everything they do has an impact on the plants and other animals living around them. A community of organisms living together and interacting is called an ecosystem, and the study of ecosystems is known as ecology. Ecologists trace the connections within natural communities. The strongest links are food chains, which show what an animal eats and which other animals prey on it. Food chains link together to form a network called a food web. If one animal in the food web becomes endangered, it can affect the rest of the ecosystem, with some animals getting rarer and others going up in number.

SURVIVAL FACTORS
Ecologists study an ecosystem in terms of factors influencing the survival of animals and plants. Major factors are the supply of food and the level of threat from predators. Other factors are the effects of the climate and seasons, and the soil conditions for plants. Zoo animals live in artificial surroundings, so keepers try to re-create features of their wild ecology. This fruit bat has melon chunks hanging in its cage so it can search for food like it would in the wild.

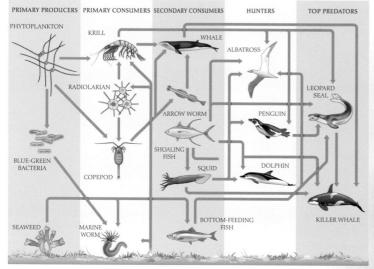

PRIMARY PRODUCERS   PRIMARY CONSUMERS   SECONDARY CONSUMERS   HUNTERS   TOP PREDATORS

PHYTOPLANKTON · KRILL · WHALE · ALBATROSS · RADIOLARIAN · ARROW WORM · LEOPARD SEAL · PENGUIN · SHOALING FISH · BLUE-GREEN BACTERIA · COPEPOD · SQUID · DOLPHIN · SEAWEED · MARINE WORM · BOTTOM-FEEDING FISH · KILLER WHALE

COMPLEX COMMUNITY
Some of the most complicated food webs are found in the oceans. As on land, the food web always begins with plants and bacteria, which harness the energy in sunlight to make their food. These are producers, and they are consumed by small animals, or primary consumers. Larger animals then prey on these primary consumers, with some species eating both plants and animals. The web continues up to the top predators. These animals have no enemies, but they rely on all the members of the food web below them for their survival.

UPS AND DOWNS
This lynx is about to catch a snowshoe hare. The lynx will eat more hares through the winter and give birth to kittens in the spring. The lynx population will then rise. However, the hare population will have dropped, so there will be less food for the lynx kittens. Some will starve to death. Now there are fewer lynx to hunt the hares, so the hare population rises. In a healthy ecosystem, these changes are normal and balance each other out over time.

POPULATION EXPLOSION

Some animals undergo sudden population changes. Locusts are good examples. Most of the time, adult locusts are plain green grasshoppers. However, when their population increases, they mature into black and yellow adults with long wings. These adults are built for swarming. Clouds of locusts containing billions of insects set off in search of plant food. These swarms can destroy a field of crops in minutes, eating up to 100,000 tons of food in a day. In 1988, a swarm even crossed the Atlantic from Africa and found food on the Caribbean islands.

Only a handful of lions can survive in the ecosystem

Wildebeest survive in huge herds

Plants make up most of the ecosystem

LIVING SPACE

Different members of an ecosystem require different amounts of space to find the food they need. Grazing herbivores such as sheep can find plant food growing all around them. A generalist such as a raccoon (see page 11) must search for its food, but it eats most things it finds and so needs a home range about half a mile (1 km) across. However, a pack of gray wolves must patrol an area of almost 80 sq miles (200 sq km) to find enough prey. Most packs have about 12 wolves.

LEVELS OF ENERGY

Living things require a supply of energy. This comes from food, which provides fuel and raw materials for building up and maintaining the body. At every stage in a food chain, some energy is lost as body heat, so there is less fuel available for the next level of animals in the chain. As a result, there are always more animals lower down the food chain than at its top. The most numerous animals are herbivores, which eat plants for hours on end each day. Predators must work hard for every meal, and they are always rare, whether endangered or not.

Measuring risk

EW	Extinct in the Wild
CR	Critically Endangered
EN	Endangered
VC	Vulnerable
NT	Near Threatened
LC	Least Concern

ON THE LIST
Every species on the Red List is given a category. About 700 animals are listed as Extinct—there is nothing we can do for them. Extinct in the Wild means a species survives only in zoos. Critically Endangered species cling on in the wild, in tiny numbers. Endangered animals have larger populations, but are still at risk. Vulnerable animals will soon become Endangered if not protected. Near Threatened species are not in danger, but could be soon. Meanwhile, species of Least Concern appear to be safe—for now.

ANIMALS ARE ENDANGERED in all corners of the world, and conservationists from different countries have to work together to save wildlife. At least 35,000 animal species need protection in some way, but which ones are most in danger? A catalog of endangered animals, plants, and fungi is produced by the International Union for Conservation of Nature (IUCN). Every year, it publishes a Red List of threatened species. This is the best guide we have to which animals are at risk of extinction. The headquarters of the IUCN are near Geneva, Switzerland, but the organization is made up of more than 1,000 conservation groups from around the world, such as Birdlife International and the National Geographic Society. These member groups work to keep the Red List database up to date.

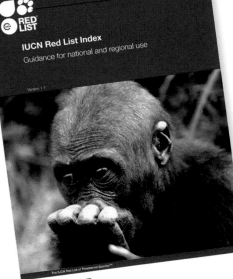

Red List logo

ALWAYS KEEPING WATCH
The Red List is updated every year as more is discovered about the state of the planet's wildlife. So far, experts have checked 47,000 species. Most of them have been added to the list, and year after year the number of threatened species goes up. This is not just because human activities are causing ever more problems for wildlife. There are at least 1.5 million more species to check. It will not be a surprise if many of these unchecked animals are also found to be endangered. Sadly, one of the first things that has to be done once a new species of animal has been studied is to figure out how to stop it from becoming extinct.

EXPERTS AT WORK
The IUCN relies on hundreds of experts to provide information on different groups of endangered animals. Project Seahorse is an international conservation team that works to protect seahorses and their relatives, such as pipefish and sea dragons. Project Seahorse scientists have made many discoveries along the way, including the fact that the mating pairs of many types of seahorse stay together for life.

FINDING GOOD NEWS
The Red List does not only tell us how bad things are. For many years, the African elephant was listed as Vulnerable. Its population shrank year after year as poachers killed the giant animals for their ivory tusks. In 1989, selling ivory was banned, but the danger remained. In 1996, the elephants became Endangered. However conservation programs eventually began to work, and by 2008 African elephants were recategorized as Near Threatened.

BEHIND THE NUMBERS

Endangered animals are not just those with small populations. Green turtles are listed as Endangered even though there are tens of thousands of them in the oceans. Turtles can live for many years so there could be plenty of turtles for some time yet. However, female turtles are producing far fewer babies each year. They cannot find enough safe beaches to dig nests for their eggs. If the turtles cannot reproduce, then their species is doomed.

COMPILING THE LIST

The Red List is not perfect. For example, every species of mammal and bird has been checked, but only 0.5 percent of insects and other invertebrates have made the list. Most endangered species are insects, but only a fraction are listed in the Red List, such as this Queen Alexandra's birdwing—the largest butterfly in the world, with a wingspan of 16 in (31 cm).

Males have colorful wings

Queen Alexandra's birdwing butterfly

HELP ARRIVES

Even if an animal is rare in one place, it may not be protected if it is common elsewhere. The bullfinches on Portugal's Azores islands were originally a subgroup of the Eurasian bullfinch. They were left unprotected even though just a few hundred lived in a patch of forest on the island of São Miguel. The Azores bullfinch was declared a species in its own right in 1993, and by 2000 it was added to the Red List. The birds were then protected by Portuguese law, and the government is now teaching schoolchildren about this special bird.

Ring identifies the bird and helps study it

COLD WAR

Recognizing the threat to rare animals can be the subject of political argument. The IUCN listed polar bears as Vulnerable 25 years ago, but the US and Canadian governments disagreed. This could be partly because some people in the Arctic rely on polar bear hunting for their livelihoods. Conservation groups finally forced the US government to protect Alaskan polar bears in 2008, but polar bear hunting is still allowed in Canada.

Watching animals in action

It is often simple to figure out how best to look after endangered animals. We can make it illegal to hunt the particular species and make sure its habitat is protected. However, it is not always clear why a species is getting rarer. Conservation relies heavily on scientists studying animal life in the wild. Sometimes they discover a keystone species, which is essential for an ecosystem's survival. For example, sea otters live in kelp forests along the North American Pacific coast and feed on sea urchins. The otters were hunted for their fur and their numbers went down. This led to an increase in sea urchins and they began eating more seaweed, killing the kelp forests. This affected sea lions, which used the underwater forests as a hiding place from sharks. The kelp forests were also a natural barrier against storms. Without them, large waves began to wash away the Pacific coast beaches—all because too many sea otters were hunted.

UP CLOSE AND PERSONAL

The first step in researching an animal is simply to watch it. Jane Goodall is an English zoologist who spent 25 years living in Tanzania and studying chimpanzees. She discovered that chimps made simple tools for collecting food, and her observations revealed a lot about how ape society works. Chimp populations are falling all over Africa, but thanks to Goodall's work we are learning about raising chimp communities in zoos until it is safe to release them into the wild again.

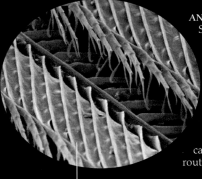

ANALYZING FEATHERS

Scientists can map where a bird has lived by studying a single feather. Special types of carbon and nitrogen atoms are found in varying amounts around the world. These atoms are in all living things, including the bird's food. The atoms are laid out along the feather according to where the bird was eating when that section of feather was growing. Researchers can use this information to follow the route taken by the bird during migration.

Feather barbs made from branching protein fibers.

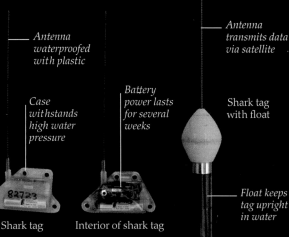

Antenna waterproofed with plastic

Antenna transmits data via satellite

Case withstands high water pressure

Battery power lasts for several weeks

Shark tag with float

82723

Shark tag

Interior of shark tag

Float keeps tag upright in water

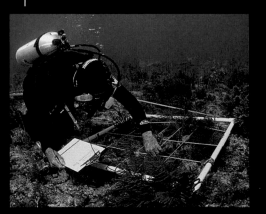

SURVEY GRID

Studying the populations of small animals takes a lot of patience. There may be hundreds of different animals packed into a tiny area. Biologists pinpoint where they all are by using a quadrat. This is a meter frame that is divided into a grid of squares. This diver is using a quadrat to survey the seafloor. He is counting the different plants and animals living in each square of the grid.

UNDERWATER TAGS

Birds, fish, and whales that travel huge distances every year may have radio tags fitted to record their journeys. The tag shown here is designed for large sharks. A harpoon dart attaches it to the shark's back. The electronics inside continuously measure depth, water temperature, and light levels. The tag is programmed to release itself from the shark on a specific date and float to the water's surface. It then transmits the information it has collected to researchers.

SMART CAMERAS

It is not always possible to watch wild animals. They may be too shy and run away from people, or they may be too few in number. Nocturnal animals, which are active only at night, are especially difficult to observe. Scientists trap the animals instead—with a camera. They set up camera traps to capture images of these nighttime creatures. The traps have motion sensors, like those used in home burglar alarms, that activate the camera when an animal walks past. This is a camera-trap image of an endangered snow leopard in Ladakh in the Indian Himalayas.

SPOT ON!

Telling the difference between animals of the same species is not always easy. Researchers look for ways of identifying individual animals so they can record how long they live, where they go, and who they mate with. Whale sharks have a unique pattern of spots on their backs, but it is impossible for the human eye to tell one pattern from another. So researchers record each whale's spots using software first developed by NASA to see patterns in the stars.

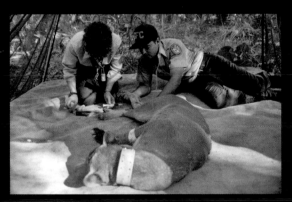

GENETIC LINKS

It is important for rare animals to breed with the best mates available. With so few mates around, it is all too easy for them to have babies with a close relative, which would lead to weak offspring. Here, animal control workers have tranquillized a Florida panther—a rare type of mountain lion—and are taking a blood sample from it. The sample will be used to identify relatives of this panther in the same area.

NEW DISCOVERIES

Sometimes field research can lead to the discovery of new species. The gray-faced sengi, a mammal living in the forests of Tanzania, was discovered in 2008 with the help of camera traps. This insect-eating animal is just 12 in (30 cm) long and lives in two small patches of protected forest in the Udzungwa Mountains.

Going, going, gone

D**URING THE LONG HISTORY OF LIFE ON EARTH,** it is not unusual for animals to become extinct. Most of the species that evolved on our planet are now gone. We know about these animals from their fossils—the hardened remains of bones and other body parts preserved in rock over millions of years. Until scientists began to study fossils about 150 years ago, people did not know that a species could die out completely. We now know that extinction is a part of evolution, as new groups of animals take over from older types. However, people cause unnatural extinctions, too. Sometimes this is on purpose, such as the wiping out in 1980 of the smallpox virus—a disease-causing agent that had killed millions of people. Extinctions have also been caused by people not caring about what they do to animals.

Leg bones were spread into a fin used for swimming

CLUES IN THE ROCK
People once thought that giant stone skulls and bones found buried in the ground belonged to dead dragons or other monsters from legends. Then, in the 1840s, fossil hunters began to uncover whole skeletons. This showed that some fossil animals were giant reptile species. Many of the extinct reptiles were named dinosaurs, meaning "terrible lizards." This skeleton is of a plesiosaur, a relative of the dinosaurs that hunted in the oceans about 200 million years ago.

Raised shell frees neck to reach leaves on tall bushes

LONESOME GEORGE
As Charles Darwin saw for himself when he visited the Galápagos Islands in 1835, each island has its own subspecies of giant tortoise. The subspecies found on Pinta Island has only one member left—Lonesome George. There are no females remaining on Pinta for George to mate with and produce the next generation. Scientists think that some Pinta tortoises were moved to other islands, and they are still searching for a female tortoise. But George can wait. He is only about 80 years old, and should live to the age of 150.

Martha, the last ever passenger pigeon

PASSAGE TO EXTINCTION
Passenger pigeons once flocked in their millions across North America, until people started to hunt them for meat. The pigeons were also hit by diseases from Europe, and they struggled to find nesting sites as forests were cut down in the 19th century. By 1870, the number of these pigeons was going down fast. The last wild bird was seen in 1900, and on September 1, 1914, Martha, the last passenger pigeon in captivity, died in the Cincinnati Zoo.

LOSING GROUND

Endangered animals are today being squeezed into smaller living areas. They may disappear completely from one part of the world—this is known as local extinction. Today, most cheetahs live in Africa, and even there they are endangered. A tiny population also survives in the deserts of Iran, but the cheetah is extinct elsewhere in Asia. The last wild Indian cheetahs were shot in 1947. A few hundred years before that, these fast-running cats were so common in India that they were trained to hunt deer. The mighty emperor Akbar had 1,000 such hunting cheetahs.

A trained hunting cheetah

LIFE IN A CAGE

The rarest animals are kept safe in zoos in case they do not survive in their natural habitat. The Brazilian Spix's macaw has not been seen in the wild since 2000. Fewer than 100 of this species now survive—all in zoos. The accidental introduction to Brazil of so-called "killer bees" from Africa in the 1960s may be one of the reasons for their extinction in the wild. These aggressive bees kill birds that come too close to their nests.

Long flight feathers similar to those of modern birds

Fingers sticking out of the wing were used for climbing

Beak contained teeth, unlike today's birds

LIVING ON

A natural extinction does not have to be the end of a species. Every new species must evolve from an older one. When that old species becomes extinct, it lives on as the newer, daughter species. Scientists call this pseudoextinction, or false extinction. According to this idea, two-legged dinosaurs called theropods are pseudoextinct, because they evolved into birds. *Archaeopteryx* is the earliest bird we know about. It evolved about 150 million years ago, when dinosaurs still roamed the Earth.

BACK FROM THE DEAD

Some scientists have suggested that we could use genetic technology to bring extinct species back to life. Experts already know how to make copies, or clones, of some living animals. If they could collect all the genes from an extinct species, they might be able to clone that species, too. This baby woolly mammoth, named Dima, was preserved for thousands of years in the frozen tundra of the Russian Arctic. One day, it may be possible to transplant Dima's genes into the egg of a mother elephant, for the elephant to give birth to a clone of Dima.

takahe $5

NEW ZEALAND

Lost and found

STUDYING THE NATURAL WORLD does not always bring bad news. Every so often amazing discoveries are made—including finding species that were thought to have become extinct. Sometimes animals are found that were supposed to have died out millions of years ago. Scientists call this the Lazarus effect, after the Christian story about a man who is brought back from the dead. There are still many wilderness areas in the world that scientists have not had a chance to study, and these are normally where long-lost animals are rediscovered. Sometimes, local people make a discovery completely by accident. While we know for sure that many species have become extinct, there is always the chance that other lost animals may one day be found, alive and well in some corner of the world.

FOUND IN THE MOUNTAINS
The takahe, a flightless grass-eating bird, once lived throughout New Zealand, but was declared extinct in 1898. Europeans settling there introduced stoats, which found it easy to kill these slow birds. But in 1948, about 100 takahe were found surviving high in the mountains. The takahe is still rare, but some have been moved to remote islands for safety.

Coelacanth

LIVING FOSSIL
Scientists know from fossils that land animals, such as reptiles and mammals, all evolved from fish with bony, rounded fins. These lobe fins became the legs of land animals. Scientists thought this type of lobe-finned fish had been extinct for 65 million years. Then, in 1938, a fishing net caught a coelacanth in the Indian Ocean. It has lobe fins like its ancient relatives and uses them for crawling around in rocky crevices on the seabed.

UNCOVERING NEW SPECIES

When researchers check how species have been identified, they sometimes find that one species is, in fact, two. This is what happened in 2006, when the rockhopper penguin was renamed as the northern and southern species. The northern rockhopper has longer plumes on its head and lives only around a few islands in the Atlantic and Indian Oceans. The penguin population on these islands has plummeted to one-tenth of its size in 50 years, and the new species was immediately given Endangered status by the IUCN.

Northern
rockhopper penguin

- HERGÉ -
LES AVENTURES DE TINTIN

*Fold of skin,
or dewlap,
is spread out
to impress
females*

HILL MONSTER

In 1990, a hunter walking through the Hellshire Hills near Kingston, Jamaica, captured what he thought was a dragon. The creature turned out to be a giant ground iguana that had been declared extinct in the 1940s. The dry, rugged hills above Kingston are not good for farming so they have remained a small wilderness. Fewer than 100 of the lizards—which grow up to 5 ft (1.5 m) long—have survived there undisturbed among cacti and shrubs. The Jamaican iguana is far from safe though. It remains perhaps the rarest lizard on Earth.

MISSING CREATURES

Some animal enthusiasts believe there are certain unusual species that have remained undiscovered. These people call themselves cryptozoologists, *crypto* meaning "hidden." Many of the hidden animals appear only in myths. Cryptozoologists think these legends are actually ancient references to real animals. Famous hidden species include the Himalayan yeti—discovered in fiction by the children's character Tintin—and the Loch Ness monster of Scotland. However unlikely it is that these creatures exist, it is almost impossible to prove scientifically that they are mythical.

*Red crest on
male bird*

Stuffed
specimen of
an ivory-billed
woodpecker

*White stripes on
back form a triangle*

LOST WOODPECKER

The ivory-billed woodpecker is the largest woodpecker species in the United States—or so it is believed. The species might have become extinct. There have been a few apparent sightings of the woodpecker over the past 10 years, but it is hard to know for sure that the endangered species has been spotted. The pileated woodpecker is a smaller and more common American species and looks very similar to the ivory-billed bird.

A LINK TO THE PAST

The Laotian rock rat was discovered in 2005 in the mountainous jungles of Laos, Southeast Asia. The rodent confused scientists at first because it looked like both a squirrel and a rat. It was later found that the species was the only surviving member of a group of rodents called the diatomyids. Until then, it was thought that the last diatomyid had scurried through the forests some 11 million years ago.

Boom and bust

THE NUMBER OF SPECIES ON EARTH does not stay the same. Scientists studying fossils from different times in the past have learned that species gradually increase in number over millions of years. But sometimes great numbers of species are wiped out all at once. These collapses are called mass extinctions and are caused by sudden changes in the environment that make it impossible for most animals to survive. Considering that life has been slowly evolving on Earth for about 3.5 billion years, mass extinctions happen very quickly and dramatically. More than three-quarters of all animals can die out in a few thousand years—perhaps even more quickly. There have been many mass extinctions in the past. Some suggest that the damage people are doing to the natural world today is creating another mass extinction.

EXPLOSION OF LIFE
Nearly all animal groups evolved during the Cambrian Period, half a billion years ago. This increase in the variety of life is known as the Cambrian Explosion. Since then, certain animals have dominated life at different times. After the Cambrian, armored sea creatures called trilobites, whose fossils are shown above, were common. Reptiles took over during the Age of Dinosaurs. These leading groups were badly affected by mass extinctions.

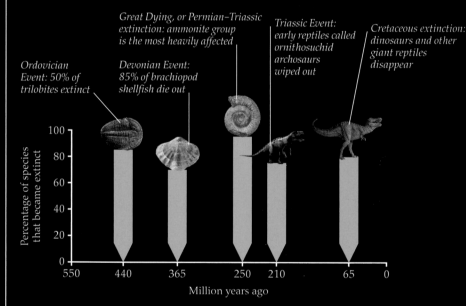

Ordovician Event: 50% of trilobites extinct

Devonian Event: 85% of brachiopod shellfish die out

Great Dying, or Permian–Triassic extinction: ammonite group is the most heavily affected

Triassic Event: early reptiles called ornithosuchid archosaurs wiped out

Cretaceous extinction: dinosaurs and other giant reptiles disappear

Percentage of species that became extinct: 0, 20, 40, 60, 80, 100

Million years ago: 550, 440, 365, 250, 210, 65, 0

THE BIG FIVE
Since the Cambrian, there have been many mass extinctions, but five catastrophes stand out as the greatest. The Ordovician Event wiped out 85 percent of species when the oceans became much shallower, killing sea life. The Devonian Event destroyed 70 percent of species, including many ancient types of fish. The next mass extinction was at the end of the Permian Period. Known as the Great Dying, it led to 96 percent of life becoming extinct. The Triassic Event 40 million years later was less severe, and probably the result of global warming. The most recent mass extinction was 65 million years ago, when all dinosaurs were wiped out.

THE GREAT DYING
The worst mass extinction we know took place 250 million years ago. Nearly all life on Earth died out. The trilobites that had survived other extinctions were wiped out, and giant armored fish called placoderms disappeared. On land, sail-backed reptiles called pelycosaurs became extinct. No one knows what caused this. One possibility is that a huge volcanic eruption in Siberia spread lava many miles thick across the land. This would have altered climates and changed habitats over the world for thousands of years.

DEATH FROM SPACE

Until the 1970s, no one had a good idea why dinosaurs suddenly became extinct. When researchers looked at rocks from the time, they found that there was a thin layer of unique dust that covered the whole planet 65 million years ago. This dust may have been produced when a 6-mile-(10-km-) wide asteroid smashed into what is now Mexico. The impact set much of the land on fire, sent giant tsunamis across the oceans, and blocked out the Sun with a dark cloud of dust and ash. The effects of such a disaster lasted for decades and spelled the end for the dinosaurs.

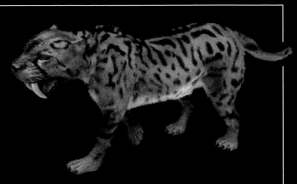

MAMMALS TAKE OVER

When dinosaurs ruled the land, mammals were small creatures. Once the dinosaurs disappeared, mammals became the dominant large animals. They grew larger and took the place of plant-eating dinosaurs. They also evolved into hunters, like this saber-toothed cat called *Eusmilus*, which preyed on the new grazing mammals.

Bony plates under the crocodile's skin armor its back

ANCIENT SURVIVOR

Some species of animal are so good at surviving that they have lived through mass extinctions. Crocodiles and alligators have seen the dinosaurs come and go. They have hardly changed in structure and in the way they live over the past 200 million years. Crocodiles are so well suited to hunting in shallow water that no other animal has been able to take over from them. When they first evolved, they preyed on reptiles and fish, but they are now just as adept at hunting birds and mammals.

The rise of humans

THE HUMAN IS THE ONLY SPECIES of animal to live on all continents of Earth. Modern humans spread out of Africa about 90,000 years ago into Asia and Europe, reaching Australia about 40,000 years ago, and the Americas about 14,000 years ago. The last continent we reached was Antarctica, where permanent bases were first set up in 1957. Humans have spread extremely quickly when compared to Earth's age. If the history of the world were represented as one calendar year, with Earth's formation on January 1, people would not appear till 11:45 p.m. on December 31. The impact of humans on Earth has been so rapid and widespread that the natural world has been struggling to cope with the changes.

Skull protects brain, which contains 100 billion nerve cells

Small cheek teeth, unlike large grinding teeth of plant-eating apes

Rib cage protects heart and lungs

Arm shorter than arm of tree-climbing ape

Flat pelvis allows for walking on two legs

Hand is free to carry objects while walking

Thumb can reach around fingers and grasp objects

Leg suited to walking long distances

Gorilla skull

Homo erectus skull

Homo sapiens skull

A NAKED APE
The closest living relatives to modern people are chimpanzees and gorillas. Our species evolved from a jungle ape that lived about 8 million years ago. Millions more years passed before the modern human species (*Homo sapiens*) evolved. Before that several other human species, including *Homo erectus*, lived in Asia, Europe, and Africa. *Homo erectus* walked like us, but was not as intelligent. *Homo sapiens* evolved about 100,000 years ago, and by 30,000 years ago, these modern humans were creating rock paintings and sculpting figurines of animals and people.

UN Secretary-General Kofi Annan holds the (symbolic) 6-billionth person in 1999

GROWING NUMBERS
While the population of many animals is falling, the human species is growing in number. The biggest rise has occurred since the 1750s, when humans learned to grow food on a large scale and cleared habitats to make room for cities and farms. Ten thousand years ago there were just 1 million humans on Earth, and by the early 1800s there were probably 1 billion. Since then, the rate of increase has risen further, due to advances in agriculture, industry, and medicine. In less than 200 years, the number jumped to 6 billion, and population experts estimate there could be 9 billion people on Earth by 2040.

World population (in billions)

6
5
4
3
2
1
0

1 CE 200 400 600 800 1000 1200 1400 1600 1800 2000
Years

RECIPE FOR SUCCESS
What makes humans so successful as a species? Compared to other animals, we cannot run very fast and are not as strong, but there is one thing we can do better—use our mental capacity. The human brain is huge for an animal of our size—three times bigger than a chimpanzee's. We use our brains to make plans, and we put them into action with our flexible hands. If we need a tool to help us, we can make one from the materials around us.

Body balanced on flattened toes

SELF-DESTRUCTION

Humans sometimes damage their habitats so much that they can no longer survive in them. Easter Island in the Pacific Ocean is famous for mysterious statues built about 600 years ago. Today, the island is covered in grass, but before people settled on it 1,000 years ago, it was a forest of palms. The islanders began to fell the trees for firewood and for building boats. A few centuries later, all the trees were gone. Without trees, the soil blew away, making farming difficult. It appears that the island's society then collapsed, with many people dying of starvation.

CAUSING EXTINCTIONS

Humans are omnivores, which means we can eat all types of food. It is likely that human hunters helped to make animals extinct in the past. For example, when the Māori people arrived in New Zealand about 1,000 years ago, they hunted the giant moas—flightless birds that stood up to 10 ft (3 m) tall. But by the 1500s, the giant moa had been hunted to extinction. The Haast's eagle, an enormous bird of prey that hunted moas, also died out because its prey had disappeared.

*Mast to which
sail was attached*

Model of Polynesian
seafaring canoe

*Double hull gave
the raft stability*

*Covered area for
people to shelter*

Giant
moa

NEW HORIZONS

Remote islands were the last places, other than Antarctica, that humans reached. Some 1,600 years ago, the Polynesian people sailed out in canoes from parts of Southeast Asia toward islands in the Pacific Ocean. They sailed huge distances by observing the stars, waves, and paths of migratory birds. Their families sailed with them, carrying animals and plants to help start a new life. Over the next 400 years, the Polynesians spread across the islands of the Pacific. Sadly, the unique wildlife on each island they reached suffered a local mass extinction.

LIVING LONGER

The population of humans is rising fast not just because more people are being born. Fewer people—especially children—are dying, too. In prehistoric times, people were lucky to make it past the age of 30. On average, an adult today will live to the age of 66, and in wealthy countries people live much longer. The increase in life expectancy is due to a better supply of good food, and high-tech medical care, which can cure diseases that would otherwise kill many of us.

The impact of farming

FOR MOST OF HUMAN HISTORY, people survived by hunting animals and gathering plant foods. Some collected the seeds, or grains, of wild wheat and barley grass for grinding into bread flour. About 10,000 years ago, people living in the Middle East made a great step forward—they learned to be farmers. Instead of traveling around to find food, farmers could settle in one place, grow wheat, and harvest grains more efficiently. Later, farmers began keeping animals, such as goats and pigs, so they stopped hunting, too. Farming allows people to create their own ecosystem, but wild animals are forced off the land and often become endangered in the process.

CROP RAIDERS
It is not just people who eat crops. Wild animals, such as these Asian elephants, often raid farms and trample entire fields. They do this because there is not enough wild habitat left to provide them with food. However, farmers need the crops to make a living, so they drive away the animals and sometimes kill them, even if they are members of an endangered species.

SLASH AND BURN
The simplest way of making a field is to cut down a patch of forest and burn the logs. This slash-and-burn technique has been a traditional farming method for thousands of years. The ash from the burned plants makes the soil fertile. However, this technique, used by these farmers in Madagascar, only works on a small scale, with the field being left to grow back into forest after a few years. Today, slash-and-burn farmers clear immense tracts of land, and the forests may never fully recover.

CROP DUSTING
Insect pests eat crops or spread plant diseases. Farmers protect their crops by spraying insecticides—chemicals that poison the insects but do not affect the crops. However, these chemicals pass up the food chain. When larger animals eat these pest insects, the poison builds up inside them. The insecticide DDT endangered hunting birds in this way (see page 42).

Insecticide sprayed from nozzles

FROM SOIL TO DUST
Most agricultural animals are grazing mammals that used to wander far and wide to find food in the wild. However, farmers often try to keep more animals than the local vegetation can support. Plant roots bind the soil, and when grazing animals in drier areas eat too many plants, the soil breaks up into dust. This dust is too loose and dry for new plants to grow in, so the fields turn into desert.

Shrimp are frozen and flown across the world

PRICE OF LUXURY
Supermarkets in wealthy countries are filled with foods grown around the world. Many foods are produced cheaply in countries where farm workers are paid low wages. New farming techniques help produce luxury foods in large amounts, but at the expense of the environment. This former mangrove swamp in Borneo has been turned into a shrimp farm. The shrimp have taken the place of the fish and birds that once lived along the coast.

A MEATY COST
Raising animals for meat requires a lot more farmland than growing plant foods. Two-thirds of all farmland is used for grazing animals. Livestock animals grow faster if they are fed rich plant food. In the US, 70 percent of grain crops are fed to animals. Raising animals for meat also uses 100 times more water than cultivating crops. As the demand for meat rises, more and more natural habitats are being cleared to make way for pastures.

Pastrami sandwich

Strong bill is good for holding prey such as frogs

FARM FRIENDLY
Some animals have benefited from farming. The cattle egret follows herds of grazing animals and snaps up insects and worms disturbed by the large animals' hooves. Cattle egrets once lived mainly in Africa, but in less than a century, they spread across Europe and traveled with imported cattle to the Americas and Australia.

SQUEEZED OUT
Some animals become endangered when the effects of farming wipe out their prey. Black-footed ferrets preyed on the prairie dogs that burrowed under the grasslands of North America, constructing intricate tunnel networks. When the grasslands became ranches, the farmers killed the prairie dogs with gas. Without prairie dogs, black-footed ferrets almost became extinct. There are now just 1,000 black-footed ferrets living in the wild. Many of them were born in zoos before being released into protected reserves.

A world without bees?

NO ONE LIKES BEING BOTHERED BY A BEE, but could we live without them? Bees, especially honeybees, are very important to our supply of fruits and vegetables. The insects collect nectar and pollen from the flowers of crop plants. They take this flower food back to the hive and use it to make a supply of honey for the whole colony. As the busy bees move from bloom to bloom, they transfer pollen grains—a process known as pollination. The pollen fertilizes the plants, allowing them to produce seeds and grow fruits. Most plants rely on bees, beetles, and other insects to pollinate them. They cannot breed without the help of visiting insects every year. However, honeybee numbers are falling fast. Wild bees have disappeared in some parts of the world. Even beekeepers are finding that their honeybee colonies are dying—and no one knows why.

HELPING HAND
Think of your favorite fruit or vegetable. The chances are it grows only after an insect has pollinated it. Hazelnuts, strawberries, onions, apples, and, in fact, all the produce shown here relies on bees for its survival. Fruits and nuts contain a plant's seeds, which grow into the next year's crop. Experts have calculated that honeybees pollinate many billions of dollars' worth of crops every year.

Pollen grains stick to the body

Bee can taste and smell with sense organs on antenna

BUSY FARM WORKERS
Farmers have always known about the link between their crops and honeybees. People have been keeping bees for at least 5,000 years. The bees were kept for their honey, but they also did a good job at keeping the fields near their hives thriving. Today, beehives are sent around the countryside to pollinate crops at the right time of year. This mobile hive in Romania contains millions of bees that will spend a few weeks working in the fields before workers move them to a neighboring farm.

WELCOME VISITOR
Flowers and bees support each other. The flower provides the insect with food, and, in return, the bee carries pollen to another plant, so it can reproduce. Honeybees prefer farms that have small fields surrounded by hedges with wildflowers, which provide food for the whole summer. However, modern farms have very large fields and any non-crop plants are weeded out. When the crops flower, the bees have a food supply, but afterward there are no other flowers around to support a colony of bees.

COLONY COLLAPSE

In the last few years, honeybees have been dying in huge numbers. The population falls so low in some hives that the colony collapses—there are not enough bees to find food and look after the young. Scientists call this problem colony collapse disorder (CCD), but they do not know its cause. Some of them think that the bees are being killed by insecticides, climate change, or radiation from cell phones. Another possibility is a virus that does not make bees sick, but stops the members of the colony from working together.

Healthy beehive with adult bees

CCD-affected beehive with fewer adult bees

Wing beats about 200 times a second during flight

URGENT MESSAGE

Keeping bees for making honey is an important industry, and colony collapse disorder is ruining many businesses. The problem has been very sudden and widespread. Beekeepers have reported problems in North America, Europe, and Asia. In some places, half of all hives have died out in just a few years. Farmers across the world are calling for scientists to study the problem before honeybees become an endangered species. These beekeepers are demonstrating outside the UK parliament.

BATTING FOR US

Besides bees and other insects, bats and birds also feed on nectar and transfer pollen, especially in warm parts of the world. Bats and birds are too heavy to land and must hover beside the flower. This lesser long-nosed bat feeding on an agave plant in Arizona has a long tongue that laps nectar. This species is now endangered because people harvest agave plants, for food and drink, before it flowers.

Flowers pollinated by bats are funnel shaped and strong smelling

Crowded out

In 2008, HUMANS became a city-based species. This was the first year in history that more people were living in cities than in the countryside. Cities cover only 3 percent of Earth's land surface—with 3 billion people crowded into them—but they have a massive effect on the environment. City dwellers do not grow their own food. That is brought in from farms—perhaps even from distant countries. So cities need roads and ports to bring in the things residents want. Cities need a constant supply of water, fuel, and power, and that often comes from outside as well. Most of the countryside has power lines and pipes running through it. A city also needs to get rid of its waste. The average resident of a European city creates 1,100 lbs (500 kg) of garbage in just one year. The growth of cities has adversely affected many animals. They are edged out of their natural habitat as cities gradually swallow up the surrounding countryside.

SHRINKING FOREST
A very special kind of tropical forest grows along the coast of Brazil. Known as the Atlantic forest, it once spread from the sandy coast up into steep mountains inland. It is home to several species of small monkey, including the golden lion tamarin, which is highly endangered. However, the forest has been cleared to make way for Brazil's largest cities, such as São Paulo and Rio de Janeiro. Today just one-tenth of the forest remains, on hilltops that are too steep to build on.

CONCRETE JUNGLE
It is often difficult to tell where a city ends and the countryside begins. Some cities have expanded to join onto a neighboring city. There are dozens of megacities with more than 10 million people living together. Big cities change the climate. Concrete and steel buildings absorb heat, making cities warmer than the surrounding countryside. Smoke and exhaust fumes combine to make an unnatural fog, or smog, seen here hanging over Shanghai, China. Smog causes breathing difficulties and can kill both people and wildlife. An immense cloud of smog often covers southern Asia in the spring. This Asian Brown Cloud, as it is known, can be seen from space.

SHOCK AND AWE

High-voltage power lines strung on towers crisscross the countryside, providing electricity for towns and cities. While it is safe for birds to perch on one wire, if they touch two wires, the electric shock kills them. Wind turbines also affect birds. The turbines are sometimes built on the same hilltops as those where large birds gather to soar upward on air currents before setting off on a migration. The birds are usually agile enough to avoid the turbine blades, but these turbines make tough migrations even harder for birds.

MAKING THE BEST OF IT

Some animals find ways to survive even in cities. Rats live in sewers, feeding on waste food, while pigeons eat whatever they can find. These animals are generalists, but some specialist animals also do well in cities. In the wild, peregrine falcons nest in cliffs, but this one finds the ledge of a skyscraper just as good. City-dwelling falcons swoop into the streets to grab pigeons.

NIGHT OR DAY?

When the Sun sets, Earth no longer goes dark. This map of Earth at night was produced using satellite images, and it shows that city lights ensure that much of Earth is lit up 24 hours a day. The lights are confusing to animals, who do not know whether the day is ending or beginning. It is not uncommon to hear birdsong in the middle of the night in cities. Birds probably mistake a streetlight for the rising Sun.

Scar on manatee's skin was caused by a boat propeller

UNDERWATER THREATS

Most of the world's biggest cities are built beside the sea. Many have harbors large enough for massive cargo ships. The noise of ship engines confuses marine mammals, such as whales and dolphins. They may swim up rivers by mistake or come too close to shore and get stuck as the tide rolls out. Most of them die. Manatees feed in shallow water around Florida. They are sometimes killed by tourist speedboats.

Warning sign protects crossing tortoises

TRAFFIC ACCIDENTS

Each year many millions of animals get squashed under the wheels of vehicles. Smaller animals, such as squirrels and raccoons, are the main victims, but sometimes, larger animals are involved. More than a quarter of a million deer are killed on the roads in the US each year. Scientists record which animals become road kill to check how common they are. For example, when fewer hedgehogs were killed on Britain's roads, it raised concerns that the animal was becoming rarer.

Damaged landscapes

A NATURAL HABITAT IS finely balanced. Even a small change caused by outside factors can have an impact on the animals living there. There are few habitats left on Earth that have escaped the effects of human activity, and damage to habitats is perhaps the main cause of animals becoming endangered. While large animals such as whales, rhinos, and tigers are at risk from direct attacks by people, many more smaller animals, such as insects, fish, and songbirds, are becoming rare because their habitats are under attack. There are two ways people damage habitats. They clear away large areas of wilderness, leaving fragments, or islands, of habitat dotted among farmland or around cities. This problem is called habitat fragmentation. The second problem is habitat degradation, where people upset the natural balance of a habitat and make life harder for the animals living there.

SHRINKING HOMELAND
Chinese alligators are smaller than their American cousins, and much rarer. These alligators used to live in vast swamps that surrounded the Yangtze River in eastern China. That habitat has been severely degraded as land is drained to make fields, and the alligators have to survive in the few muddy pools and ditches among the farms. There are fewer than 150 left in the wild. All other Chinese alligators are confined to small nature reserves.

TRAPPED IN THE TREES
Gibbons are especially affected by habitat fragmentation. These Southeast Asian apes swing from branch to branch on their enormously long arms. They cannot walk long distances across open ground, which means groups of gibbons become trapped in small fragments of forest. All the gibbons in one fragment are related to one another, and so the apes are forced to breed with their relatives. This is called inbreeding, and it creates health problems that result in fewer young growing up.

Many small plants called epiphytes may grow on a rain forest tree

RELYING ON VARIETY
Untouched habitats have more plant species than areas in the same region affected by human activity, and that means they have more animals, too. The wealth of plants provides homes for many small creatures. Insect species have often evolved alongside certain plants that supply them with food and places to lay eggs. Without these plants, the insects cannot survive. Experts believe that every time a plant species is lost from a tropical rain forest, a dozen insect species also become extinct.

HOMELESS ON THE RANGE

The Great Plains is a dry grassland area that runs down the middle of North America. This habitat is also known as the prairie, but in most places the natural prairie grasses have been replaced by wheat fields and cattle pastures. Just 200 years ago, the prairie was home to many millions of bison (right) and antelopelike pronghorns. Today, these unique North American animals number only in their thousands, and tiny patches of true prairie cover just 1 percent of the original Great Plains.

YOUNG FOREST

When a tree is cut or falls down in a forest, the gap created is filled by fast-growing shrubs and small trees. The thicket produced is called secondary forest. Given time, patches of secondary forest blend into the mature forest. However, logging and forest clearances may create so many gaps that secondary forest becomes more common than mature forest. Secondary forest has fewer plants than mature habitat. In tropical forest, it lacks the tall emergent trees that rise above the surrounding forest. Animals such as howler monkeys, which live in emergent trees, are rarer in secondary forests.

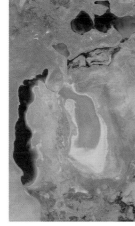

Satellite image, 1989   Satellite image, 2008

MISSING WATER

In the 1960s, the Aral Sea in central Asia was the fourth largest lake in the world. Today, most of it is desert. Almost all the river water that once fed the lake has been diverted to water cotton fields elsewhere. The Aral Sea was always salty, but it was home to 24 species of unusual river fish that could survive in the salty water. With the water increasing in saltiness as it decreases in area, only four of these original fish species survive in the remaining patches of water.

LIFE ON THE MOVE

Migrating animals visit several habitats on their journey, and every stop is crucial. The Siberian crane spends the summer in Siberia and winter in the wetlands of Iran, China, and India. But the birds have failed to arrive in India since 2002, and in 2005, only four cranes were counted in Iran. Now, the remaining Chinese population of cranes is at risk from a new dam on the Yangtze River, which will stop water reaching the bird's winter habitat.

WHAT'S IT WORTH?

There are a few places on Earth that are still untouched by humans. Much of this pristine wilderness is in the polar regions, like this area in Antarctica, where it is too cold for people to live. Nevertheless, people have been looking at ways of making money from wildernesses such as Antarctica or Alaska by drilling for oil or by mining. But conservationists argue that the land is worth much more left as it is. In 1998, the Antarctic Protocol made it illegal for anyone to damage the habitats of Antarctica. Even scientists working there must take every last scrap of their garbage back with them.

Climate change

EARTH'S CLIMATE HAS never been constant.
At different times over millions of years, natural
climate change has spread hot desert, humid
forest, or icy plains over large parts of the planet.
This natural change has caused many past
extinctions, but now it appears that humans are
changing the climate, too. We may be doing it so
fast that wildlife cannot cope with the pace of change
in their habitats. Humans are making Earth warmer
by releasing carbon dioxide and other gas pollution
into the air. An increase of just 6.3°F (3.5°C) could
cause a new mass extinction that would kill up to
70 percent of all species, including humans.

*Short wings
held close
to body*

Aldabra rail

RISING OCEANS
Water slowly expands as it gets warmer.
There is so much water in the oceans that
even a small increase in its temperature leads
to an expansion that pushes up the surface.
Melting polar ice caps will also add more water
to the oceans. No one is quite sure by how much
climate change will raise sea levels—predictions
range from 35 in (90 cm) to 29 ft (8.8 m) over the
next 100 years. Higher seas spell trouble for animals
on low-lying islands, such as Aldabra in the Indian
Ocean, which would be mostly under water.
The island's unique wildlife, such as this
flightless Aldabra rail, would be wiped
out by the rising waters.

A BURNING ISSUE
Global warming does not simply make the Earth a
little hotter. The extra heat trapped in the atmosphere
also makes the weather more extreme. Storms may
get fiercer and droughts last for longer. In recent years,
many forests around the world, dried out by lack of rain,
have been destroyed by immense wildfires. While many
forest plants can quickly thrive after small fires, large
wildfires are so hot that the forest habitats and the animal
populations within them will take decades to recover.

DISAPPEARING ICE

The polar bear is built for hunting on the frozen Arctic Ocean. The bear's pale coat makes it hard to spot on the ice, and the blanket of hairs keep the bear's skin warm and dry. The bear even has hairs insulating the soles of its feet—they also act as grips on the slippery ice. Polar bears hunt for seals and seabirds, mostly at the edge of the ice. However, global warming is making sea ice melt faster each year, forcing polar bears to hunt on land. The bear is now classified as Endangered, and if the Arctic Ocean melts completely, it could become extinct.

STOKING THE FIRES

Human-made climate change is the result of people burning coal, gasoline, and natural gas. These are called fossil fuels because they formed from forests and sea life that were buried millions of years ago. When we burn these fuels today in power plants or car engines, we release carbon dioxide that had been locked away underground for all that time. The extra carbon dioxide in the air traps the Sun's heat, making Earth hotter. In the last 200 years, humans have increased the amount of carbon dioxide in the atmosphere by 40 percent.

Bleached coral has turned white

Painted lady feeding on a flower

CHANGING SCENE

The effects of climate change can already be seen by the shifts in where certain animals live. Apollo butterflies live in cool alpine meadows in Europe. Climate change is making these meadows less common, and so the apollo has been listed as Vulnerable. However, painted lady butterflies from warmer climates are doing better. They migrate from North Africa and the Mediterranean to northern Europe in summer, and most used to die as winter set in. Warmer weather means that today, painted ladies can survive all year round in some areas of northern Europe.

ACID ATTACK

The increased level of carbon dioxide in the atmosphere is affecting the oceans. It dissolves in water to form carbonic acid—the same thing that puts bubbles in carbonated drinks. The warmer the oceans get, the more acidic they become. Corals grow in warm waters, but the increase in ocean temperature and acidity is killing coral reefs. The tiny algae that live inside the corals providing them with food, die away. As a result, the corals become bleached white and may die. In the Indian Ocean, about 90 percent of corals have been bleached.

COMBATING CLIMATE CHANGE

The problem of climate change has been accepted by most governments of the world. There are many ideas about how to tackle it. The most important thing is finding new ways to generate power without burning fossil fuels. However, a rescue plan will work only if all countries work together. Former US vice-president Al Gore is one of the leading voices urging an international agreement. Despite time running out, no climate change treaty has yet been agreed upon.

Global amphibian decline

AMPHIBIANS ARE THE OLDEST group of land vertebrates, or animals with backbones. They evolved from fish about 375 million years ago. Since that time, mass extinctions have wiped out all the larger types of amphibian—the surviving members of the group are frogs, toads, newts, salamanders, and wormlike caecilians. There are almost 6,000 species of amphibian today, but one-third of them are at risk of extinction. That makes them the most threatened animals on Earth. The crisis facing the world's amphibians is called the "global amphibian decline." Amphibians live in water and on land and are exposed to pollution in both their habitats. Many people think amphibians are dying out because they are being hit twice by environmental damage. The global amphibian decline could be a warning of what awaits other animal groups in the future.

Skin must be damp so body doesn't dry out

WATER, WATER EVERYWHERE
Most amphibians must return to water to mate and lay their eggs. Some lay their eggs in ponds, while others lay them in rain puddles or even tiny pools trapped in leaves. Starting life in water puts amphibians at great risk from pollution and drought. In some warm, wet parts of the world, frogs breed throughout the year, laying a small number of eggs at a time. In cooler areas, frogs have a breeding season and lay huge numbers of eggs all at once. Seasonal breeding carries high risks because an entire generation of eggs can be killed in one go.

Each egg is protected by a coat of jelly

Thin skin on belly absorbs most water

Red-eyed tree frog of Costa Rica

Sticky toe pad lets feet cling to flat surfaces

LIVING WITHOUT LUNGS
Lungless salamanders live almost entirely in damp forests in North and Central America. These amphibians do not have lungs but breathe by absorbing oxygen through their skin. Many lungless salamanders do not start life in water like other amphibians. Their eggs are laid on land and the babies hatch out looking like tiny adults. However, the salamanders' forests are being cleared rapidly, putting about 200 lungless species at risk of extinction.

IN CLOSE TOUCH

Frogs can breathe through their skin. It is thin enough for oxygen to pass through, especially in the lining of the throat. Other chemicals can travel into the body through the skin, and frogs can also taste with it. It is easy for even tiny amounts of pollution to get into a frog's body, which is another probable cause for their global decline. Sadly, it makes amphibians good biological indicators—they can alert us when a problem is developing in a habitat.

FUNGUS ATTACK

Another problem facing amphibians is a deadly fungus. The chytrid fungus lives in an amphibian's sensitive skin and makes it so sore that it can no longer move around to feed or to escape attack. The fungus is thought to have come from Africa and is being spread around the world by a few resistant species, such as African clawed toads, cane toads, and bullfrogs. Today, the fungus is attacking native amphibians almost everywhere. Only Asia has, so far, escaped the problem.

Microscope image of chytrid fungus growing in a salamander's skin

Folds on skin allow for more absorption of oxygen from water

LARGEST OF THE LOT

The Chinese giant salamander is the largest species of amphibian alive today. It grows to 6 ft (1.8 m) and lives in mountain streams, where it feeds on fish and frogs. Chinese salamanders are naturally rare because there are few places where such a large creature can survive. However, the giant is also critically endangered because it is hunted for its meat and for use in traditional Chinese medicine. In the last 30 years, the population of the giant salamander has shrunk by 80 percent.

TOAD TUNNEL

Frogs and toads often return to breed in the pool where they hatched. They sniff out their pond and will stop at nothing to get there during the breeding season. If a road lies across the route to the pool, the slow-moving frogs will hop across it, with many being killed by traffic. To protect rare amphibians, such as natterjack toads, road builders sometimes construct a tunnel under the road so they can cross safely.

Rivers in crisis

LIFE WOULD NOT EXIST without water. Land animals need fresh water, provided by rainfall and melting mountain snow and ice, to stay alive. The water travels across the land in streams and rivers, which form an intricate web of changing habitats as they flow to the ocean. Clear streams gushing down rocky hills are very different from muddy rivers that mix with seawater at the coast, but animals survive in all of these habitats. Rivers are also important to people. The most heavily populated parts of Earth have grown around great rivers. People take water out of rivers, pollute them, change their courses, and dam them in places, all of which threaten the aquatic animals living there.

RIVER DOLPHINS
Several types of dolphin regularly swim up rivers from the ocean, but three species are special because they live only in fresh water and never leave their rivers. The boto lives in the Amazon, the south Asian river dolphin lives in the Ganges, Brahmaputra, and Indus rivers, while the baiji (shown above) lives in the Yangtze in China. All river dolphins are endangered, but the baiji may already be extinct in the wild. The Yangtze is a very busy and polluted watercourse, and there has been only one possible sighting of a wild baiji since 2002. If the baiji is indeed lost, it will be the first dolphin species to be made extinct by human activity.

BANKING ON RIVERS
Gharials are fish-eating crocodilians that live in south Asia. They have short legs and cannot walk well. When not swimming, gharials slither onto sandbanks in the middle of the river. There are only about 200 gharials left in the wild. Hunters have almost wiped them out over the past 60 years, but today the gharials face a host of other threats. Crop irrigation drains the water out of the gharials' rivers in the dry season, water released from dams can wash young ones away, fishermen accidentally catch them in their nets, and sand taken away for construction means there are fewer places for the gharials to rest.

WATERING CROPS
River water is used to turn dry land into lush fields. Irrigation projects have transformed much of the western United States, Australia, and central Asia into fertile farmland. So much water is taken from the Colorado River to water crops and feed cities in the American West that the mighty river is reduced to a trickle by the time it reaches the ocean. Pumping water onto the dry land also causes problems. Salts build up in the soil, making it harder to grow crops there.

NO WAY HOME

Salmon make epic journeys up rivers, swimming inland from the ocean to mate and lay eggs (spawn). They seek out the same river in which they themselves hatched. If the fish cannot reach their spawning ground, they die trying. Salmon can leap over waterfalls and other natural obstacles, but they cannot pass giant dams. The Columbia River system in the US's Pacific Northwest has 11 dams used as power plants. Some of the dams have salmon ladders—a staircase of pools—for the fish to climb up, but several rivers are blocked completely. The salmon that spawned there are now sadly extinct. Lonesome Larry, the last salmon in Redfish Lake, Idaho, died in 1992.

MUDDY WATERS

A healthy river is filled with useful nutrients that flow into the sea. However, cutting down forests around the river can make it a destructive force. Tree roots hold soil together and help it soak up water. When the trees are cut down, the loose soil is washed into the river, making the water dark and muddy. The mud clogs up the river downstream, killing water plants and the animals that eat them. Deforestation also causes flooding. Heavy rain that was once absorbed by trees and soil now flows straight into the river, creating a dangerous surge of water.

Mature male gharial has a bulge at the end of his long, narrow snout

Mussel lives inside hinged shell

FILTERED OUT

Mussels filter their food from water, so every impurity the water contains passes through their bodies. River species, such as the endangered freshwater pearl mussel, are often the first to be affected by pollution. Dams also threaten shellfish. A dammed river gets deeper and covers the shallow rapids where mussels once thrived. As a result, shellfish make up one of the most endangered groups of animals, with about 250 species becoming extinct in the last 100 years.

PUMP AND DUMP

Many rivers are used as dumping grounds. Sewage and other waste is pumped into the water, from where it flows downstream. The pollution ranges from chemical poisons to less dangerous substances such as crop fertilizer, and even hot water. But fertilizers and heat make water plants grow faster, and they form a green scum on the surface that blocks out light. Most fish and other animals in the dark water beneath then find it tough to survive.

Polluted world

Normal peregrine falcon egg

DDT-poisoned peregrine falcon egg

ONE OF THE THINGS THAT sets humans apart from the rest of the animal kingdom is that we create pollution. Pollution is anything that has been added to the environment and that is poisonous or harmful to wildlife and people alike. Pollution spreads through the air, water, and soil, and no place on Earth is free from it. Litter is scattered across the deep seabed and dangerous artificial chemicals have been found frozen in Antarctic ice. The most damaging are poisonous chemicals that kill plants and create health problems in animals. However, just about anything can cause pollution. For example, carbon dioxide is produced naturally by all plants and animals. Industries release excess carbon dioxide into the environment, so this harmless gas becomes a pollutant. Controlling pollution is a key part of saving endangered animals.

BREAKING EGGS
In the 1950s, people used a chemical called DDT to kill pest insects. The pesticide did its job well. Once it had been sprayed, it stayed in the soil for weeks. Eventually, the DDT was washed away. However, it did not disappear—the chemical got into the food chain when animals ate affected insects. Scientists thought DDT was harmless to vertebrates, but the chemical then built up in the bodies of predators, especially birds of prey. DDT made the birds' eggs fragile so they broke before chicks could hatch. DDT poisoning made many hunting birds, such as peregrine falcons, highly endangered in some countries.

Sensitive eyes can see well in water

LIGHTS IN THE SKY
Pollution can also be caused by light and noise. Light pollution can confuse animals that have evolved to live in the dark of night. For example, baby sea turtles hatched from eggs buried on sandy beaches find their way to the ocean by looking for moonlight reflecting off the water. However, if they see an artificial light on the shore, they head the wrong way and get lost. Many babies do not reach the water, and light pollution is one of the reasons why sea turtles are so endangered.

PLASTIC IS NOT FANTASTIC
Plastic does not decay in the same way as natural materials, such as wood or paper. Huge amounts of plastic—bags, bottles, containers, lighters—end up in the ocean and float there for years, slowly releasing poisons into the water. The plastics are swept by ocean currents into massive litter fields. The Great Pacific Garbage Patch—containing millions of tons of plastic—is spread out across the ocean between Japan and California. Plastic fragments are dangerous for animals. This albatross chick has died because its parents kept feeding it plastic garbage, mistaking the plastic for food.

Rescuers keep whale's skin damp while waiting for high tide

TOO MUCH NOISE
Noise pollution is a particular problem in the ocean. Sound travels long distances in water, and some animals, such as whales, communicate by singing to one another. Others bounce echoes off the coast and seabed to help them find their way. The sound from ship engines and submarine sonars may have confused this pilot whale, forcing it to become stranded on the coast of Australia. Its pod (group) of about 80 whales came too close to the shore in 2009, then got stuck on the beach when the tide went out. The heavy whales cannot survive long out of the water. Rescuers helped some back into the ocean, but 70 of the whales died from exhaustion.

VANISHING VULTURES

Vultures are seen as valued natural cleaners. They pick clean the carcasses of dead cattle—and even dispose of human bodies in some Indian funeral traditions. However, India's three vulture species have almost been wiped out over the past 20 years. The cause is diclofenac, a painkilling drug given to sick farm animals. The drug passes into the vultures' bodies, and even small amounts are enough to kill the birds.

AIR WAYS

Biologists have discovered that countless tiny animals are blown along by the wind. These are not just the bugs that get squashed on car windshields, but tiny insects, such as thunderflies and aphids, and ballooning spiders, which catch the wind with trails of silk. This aerial plankton has no control of where it ends up, but the small animals use the wind to spread themselves to new places. Sadly, it appears that aerial plankton is being thinned out due to smog and other air pollution. In many countries, a windshield splattered with bugs is a thing of the past.

OIL AND WATER DON'T MIX

Some of the biggest pollution disasters are oil slicks, created when millions of gallons of crude oil are spilled from gigantic oil tankers. The thick oil floating on the surface of the ocean blocks out the light and stops oxygen from mixing into the water. Many animals beneath the giant slick struggle to survive. The oil also damages the feathers of seabirds, preventing the birds from flying and finding food, so many die. The slicks are hard to clear up, especially if they wash onto the shore. Oil pollution can damage coastal habitats for decades.

Oil sticks to bird's feathers and strips off waterproofing

Wildlife for sale

Before humans started farming, they killed wild animals for food and made clothes and tools from their skins and bones. In prehistoric times, human hunters were the same as any other predator. They had to work hard to make kills, and if there was no prey, they starved. Over the years, hunting techniques became more efficient, and people were able to hunt on a large scale. Later, animals were hunted for sport, as humans tested themselves against other fierce predators. Hunting also became an industry, with furs, horns, and other exotic animal products being sold across the world. Inevitably, hunting drove some species to extinction, and people realized that many more were close to the brink. Today, most countries have laws that protect rare animals from hunters, but sadly, criminals and poachers still kill endangered species and sell their body parts for high prices.

Tine (prong) growing from main antler

TROPHY HUNTING
Hunters like to show off their kills as trophies, and some seek out the largest and most dangerous game. In the past, wealthy hunters traveled to Africa to shoot lions, elephants, and antelopes, and tourists still pay large fees to hunt African animals. Big game hunting can help pay for nature reserves as long as it is properly controlled. Reserve managers give strict instructions about which animals can be shot. For example, they make sure female animals raising young are protected so the overall wildlife population is not affected. Sometimes widespread hunting is allowed, to keep the population of a species in check, as with the sika deer in northern Japan.

Hunter stands on pile of bison skulls

MASS SLAUGHTER
Before humans reached North America, there were around 100 million bison living on the continent. By the 1830s, armed Native American hunters on horseback were shooting up to 250,000 bison each year. When European settlers reached America's Great Plains, they began to slaughter the bison in even greater numbers. By 1890, only about 1,000 bison remained. Today, there are 15,000 bison, but few live wild like their ancestors.

Wall-mounted trophy of a sika deer

Pangolin (left) and baby antelope for sale in Lagos, Nigeria

BANNED ANIMAL GOODS
The body parts of rare animals are ingredients in some traditional Asian medicines. Although there is little evidence that the medicines do any good, there is a high demand for them, especially in China. Rhinos, tigers, and seahorses are a few of the animals that have become severely endangered because their bones and organs are sold for use in Chinese medicine. Although they are on sale in this store in Myanmar, trading any part of an endangered animal is against the law in most countries.

LUXURY AT ANY PRICE
Caviar—the eggs of sturgeon fish—is the ultimate luxury food. The rarest and costliest caviar is taken from the 20-ft (6-m) beluga sturgeon, which lives in the Caspian and Black Seas. To harvest caviar, fishermen must catch female fish before they lay their eggs. As a result, the fish do not get a chance to breed. The sturgeon population has gone down so rapidly that catching the fish is banned in most places. However, a pound of beluga caviar fetches $7,500, so many fishermen break the ban.

Fresh caviar

BUSHMEAT
Despite international laws and conservation programs, one threat is hard to protect against—people eating local wild animals. A wild animal sold as food is called bushmeat. Many people are too poor to buy farmed meat, and so they eat bushmeat instead. However, in some cultures bushmeat is highly prized, and people prefer to eat wild animals. Many animal species are eaten, including rare monkeys and apes. Bushmeat is most common in west and central Africa, where it is a major threat to highly endangered chimps and gorillas.

ANIMAL SLAVES
Animals are also sold when they are alive. Circuses often put animals on display, but endangered species such as tigers and bears are rarely seen today. Dancing bears were commonly made to perform in eastern Europe and southern Asia, and although this cruel practice is dying out, it persists in a few places. Other animals, especially monkeys and apes, are still taken from the wild and sold as playthings.

Sloth bear being forced to perform

CAGED FOR LIFE
People who keep exotic pets may seem like animal lovers, but the unusual animals have often been captured from the wild. The international pet trade causes additional problems for many birds, reptiles, amphibians, and fish already threatened by habitat loss. Many of these animals die on their long journeys to pet stores around the world. It is against the law to buy endangered animals, even as pets. These endangered golden conures were collected illegally from a rain forest in Brazil.

Sharks in peril

SHARKS ARE AMONG the most feared of animals. Attacks on people are, in fact, very rare, but when they happen they are truly terrifying, as the monster fish suddenly appears from the deep sea. However, our fear of sharks can make us forget that many of them are highly endangered. Sharks (and their relatives, the rays) form one of the most ancient animal groups. They have been hunting in the oceans for some 370 million years, but today about half of all sharks and ray species are in danger. While big sharks can pose a real danger to humans, many sharks are quite small in size, and we are much more of a threat to them. About 60 people get attacked by sharks every year, and perhaps six of them die. However, humans kill many thousands of sharks every single day.

SHARK IN YOUR SOUP
Shark fin soup is a popular dish in eastern Asia. Every year, fishermen catch 38 million sharks just for their fins. They target medium-sized species such as tiger, blacktip, and mako sharks. In many cases, a captured shark is tossed back into the water once its three main fins are cut off. The finless shark is still alive, but now cannot swim and so sinks to its death. Bizarrely, the fin meat is quite tasteless and could easily be replaced with another ingredient.

Strong reel

Large shark hook

Sturdy fishing rod

BATTLING SHARKS
Some sport fishermen like to catch the largest and most dangerous fish they can find, and as a result they kill half a million sharks every year. Part of the appeal is to have a photo taken back on shore showing off the size of the catch. However, more and more boat marinas are banning people from landing dead sharks on their docks, in the hope that fewer fishers will target these threatened animals.

DEATHLY NETS
One of the biggest threats to sharks comes from fishing nets. Millions of sharks become tangled in nets by accident each year. The trapped shark cannot breathe properly, and it is usually dead by the time the net is hauled out of the water. Many tourist beaches are also protected by anti-shark nets. Sharks often cannot see these barriers clearly until it is too late. In future, shark nets may be equipped with electronic warning devices. These will give out electric pulses that only sharks can detect, and which will drive the animals away before they become trapped in the net.

Dusky shark caught in anti-shark net off South African coast

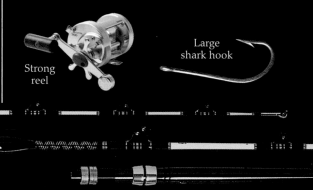

ENDANGERED GIANT
The whale shark is the largest fish in the world. It can grow as long as a bus, but it is not a fierce hunter—it feeds on plankton and small fish. The whale shark is one of the most endangered shark species. In 2002, it was made illegal to catch one, but fishermen still sometimes sell giant whale shark fins for high prices. Before the trade ban, whale sharks were captured for giant aquariums, such as this one in Japan. However, whale sharks do not survive for long in tanks.

SHARK PLATTER

People sometimes eat shark without realizing it. Small sharks such as this spiny dogfish are given more appealing names in restaurants. For example, in the UK, shark meat is served in fish-and-chip restaurants as rock salmon or huss. In Belgium, it is called sea eel. However, the spiny dogfish is listed by the IUCN as Vulnerable. In the waters around Europe, 90 percent of these little sharks have disappeared due to overfishing.

UNFAIR FEAR

Many people's dread of sharks comes from the way these animals are shown in movies like *Jaws* and *Deep Blue Sea*. In these films, sharks are frightening monsters that will stop at nothing to eat human flesh. In reality, sharks do not like eating humans. We are perhaps too bony for them—big sharks prefer to eat blubbery sea mammals. Sharks do sometimes bite people by mistake. Surfers are especially at risk, because their boards might look like a large seal to a shark. However, sharks rarely go on to eat their unfortunate human victims. They spit them out and look for tastier prey, but even a single shark bite can cause serious injury.

Shark tooth marks

Surfboard bitten in half by shark

Poster for the film *Jaws*

SLOW TO RECOVER

With an estimated 100 million sharks being killed each year, it is no surprise that the number of sharks is going down fast. Like large land animals, sharks produce only a few pups, or young, each year, so it can take many years for a normal population to grow back again. Several species, such as the fearsome great white shark, give birth to live young. Other sharks lay eggs in oblong cases, known as mermaid's purses.

Shark pup inside mermaid's purse

Alien invaders

Black rat,
or ship rat

ONE OF THE FACTORS THAT DRIVES the process of evolution is isolation. A new species may evolve when one set of animals is cut off from its relatives. Natural barriers such as deserts, mountains, and oceans divide our planet into separate regions. A snake species that evolved in South America could never meet another snake species from central Asia. But this changed when humans began exploring the globe and set up trade routes that passed around, and over, Earth's natural barriers. Animals moved with the explorers and traders. Sometimes animals hitched a ride by accident, but many other animals, such as cattle, dogs, and rabbits, were taken to new areas on purpose. Once they got there, these alien invaders soon took over, often leaving native species fighting for survival—especially on long-isolated islands.

UNWANTED PASSENGERS
Mice and rats are always on the lookout for scraps of food, and their curiosity means they can end up just about anywhere—on a ship, in a cargo container, or even aboard a plane. The rodents can normally survive very well wherever they end up. Mice and rats have killed off many native species in the course of their spread around the world. One of the first extinctions they probably caused was of the Cuban coney, another type of rodent. It was wiped out after rats were introduced to Cuba, a few years after the island had been discovered by Christopher Columbus.

DISAPPEARING WOLVES
The Ethiopian wolf is the rarest species of dog. There are barely 400 of them left in a few mountains in Ethiopia. They survive by hunting rats that burrow under the mountain meadows. The wolf's biggest threat is from domestic dogs. The dogs have introduced rabies, a disease that killed two-thirds of the wolves in Bale, their main stronghold. Some survivors bred with their domestic cousins, producing wolf-dog hybrids that may drive the wolves to extinction.

SQUIRREL WARS
Just a century ago, the most common squirrel species in the British Isles was red and had large, tufted ears. Today, gray squirrels from North America have taken over. They were introduced to the British Isles in the second half of the 19th century. The grays come from the oak forests of the eastern US and Canada, are bigger than the reds, and chase them away from prime feeding sites. Today, red squirrels are common only in areas of pine forest that are too cold for the grays. But gray squirrels are spreading, heading east through mainland Europe.

STINGERS ON THE TRAIL

One of the unfriendliest introduced species is the red fire ant. This insect is named after its painful sting—and when one stings you, it is likely that a hundred more ants will soon join in the attack. In the past 80 years, imported red fire ants have spread in cargo ships from Brazil to the southern US, Australia, the Philippines, and Taiwan. The ants damage crops and they also kill many native insects that live near the ants' large mounds.

Nile perch weighing 175 lbs (80 kg) caught in Lake Victoria

FISH HUNTER

Africa's Lake Victoria is enormous—and home to a huge number of fish. Most of the lake's 500 fish species are cichlids, which form what is known as a species flock. The little cichlids are closely related, with each species adapted to life in a particular part of the lake. However, the lake's great diversity is under threat. In 1954, the Nile perch was introduced into the lake. This big hunting fish has become a valuable source of food, but it survives by eating the cichlids. About 200 cichlid species have already become extinct.

Cat bites bird's neck

TIBBLES, THE KILLER CAT

New Zealand has a unique wildlife dominated by birds. The islands have almost no native mammals. Many of the birds are flightless, which made them easy prey for mammal predators introduced by humans over the past 1,000 years. There is a story that the rare Stephens Island wren was hunted to extinction in 1894 by a lighthouse keeper's cat called Tibbles. In truth, the little bird was wiped out by hundreds of wild cats that swarmed over the island.

GOATS VERSUS SNAKES

Round Island, a small rocky island in the Indian Ocean, is home to one of the rarest snakes in the world. There are about 1,000 Round Island keel-scaled boas left. Once there were many more of them, hunting lizards in the shrubs and trees. However, farmers cleared the island's forests and herds of goats were brought to the island to feed visiting sailors. These grazing invaders have eaten much of the remaining undergrowth that once sheltered the snakes.

Container fits on a single truck at port

ACROSS THE WORLD

The world is more connected than ever before. Giant ships carry containers filled with cargo across the world. Many objects around you will have been transported this way—and animals would have hitched a ride with them, too. Many of the stowaways are insects, hidden among food or hatching from eggs left in soil or water. Some insects carry diseases. It is possible that a disease such as the West Nile virus was introduced to North America when mosquitoes carrying the virus were transported there on cargo ships.

Fighting back

AT ONE TIME, PEOPLE did not realize that their actions could damage the natural world. Hunting was not controlled and even naturalists tended to study nature by collecting specimens they had killed. In the 1920s, two sons of US president Theodore Roosevelt went to China to collect giant pandas for the Field Museum, Chicago. They shot the bears dead. Attitudes in some countries were slowly changing, however. In Britain, as early as 1889, the Royal Society for the Protection of Birds formed in protest at the use of wild bird feathers in fashionable hats. In Africa, experts noticed declines in mammal numbers due to overhunting. They founded the conservation charity Flora and Fauna International in 1903. The environmental movement was slow to take hold, but awareness of "green" issues grew during the 20th century. Today, many countries have laws that stop people from damaging the environment.

BIG GAME
In the late 19th and early 20th centuries, wealthy hunters traveled the world to shoot big game—the biggest and often the fiercest animals to be found. Here, the future king of England, George V, poses with a tiger and two leopards shot during a visit to India in 1906. The dead animals were often stuffed as trophies—the king's tiger is still on display at a museum in Bristol, England. However, many people began to think that hunting for fun was cruel, and a threat to rare species. Today, in most countries, endangered animals cannot be hunted, and other game hunting is strictly controlled.

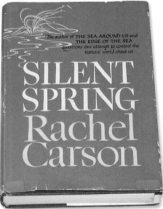

WRITTEN WARNING
In 1962, American author Rachel Carson published *Silent Spring*. The title hinted at how humans were doing so much damage to the natural world that one day there would be no wildlife left. Springtime—instead of being full of bird song and other signs of life—would be dead and silent. Before Carson explained how chemicals used by farmers were poisoning nature, many people thought that high-tech agriculture could only be a good thing. *Silent Spring* changed that and made many more people interested in protecting the environment.

Poached ivory tusk cut from dead elephant

POPULAR SUPPORT

In the 1970s, protecting the environment become a political issue. People began asking politicians to make their countries more environmentally friendly, or "green." On April 22, 1970, the first Earth Day was held, and today, millions of people observe Earth Day around the world. Schoolchildren spend the day learning more about endangered animals and other green issues. The day is also a time for protests, when people try to persuade their governments to fix environmental problems. These green activists in the Philippines are protesting about pollution caused by power plants and mines in the country.

Horn of black rhino killed by poacher

AN ARMED RESPONSE

In 1975, the Convention on International Trade in Endangered Species, or CITES, banned the sale of endangered animals worldwide. However, in the case of the rarest animals, this ban had little effect, since poachers were willing to break the law to get hold of tiger bones, gorilla meat, elephant ivory, and rhino horns. The only option for governments was to back the ban with force. Today, armed rangers patrol nature reserves with orders to protect the animals at any cost.

Greenpeace speedboat prevents hunter from harpooning whales

GREEN WARRIOR

Protesting was not enough for some. The Greenpeace organization was set up in the 1970s to take direct action to save wildlife. Its members are sent to record environmental damage as it happens and to stop it from happening if they can. Greenpeace's first campaign was to stop governments from testing atom bombs that polluted the oceans with dangerous chemicals. It later began to fight against whale hunting. Thanks to Greenpeace and other campaigners, whaling was banned in 1986.

DIFFERENCES OF OPINION

There is still disagreement on how to protect endangered animals. Some say a worldwide ban on hunting is the only way to save large animals, such as the African elephant. Others say bans are only needed in places where the animals cannot be protected in other ways. When this pile of poached elephant tusks was burned in Kenya, park rangers from South Africa complained that the ivory was wasted and that it could have been sold to pay for conservation programs. In South Africa, there are so many elephants that rangers often shoot animals to prevent overcrowding. However, they are not allowed to sell the valuable skins or tusks left behind.

LETTING PEOPLE KNOW

Most animal lovers have never seen a tiger or rhino in real life. The nearest they can get to these rare creatures is by watching them on TV. Before nature documentaries brought the lives of animals into their homes, few people knew or cared much about wild animals. While TV personalities such as Bindi Irwin (right), like her late father Steve, tell us more about the threats facing wild animals, filmmakers are always working on better ways to capture the amazing sights and sounds of nature. Viewers do not like the idea of such beauty disappearing forever, so many more people are now willing to support conservation programs.

Saving habitats

STAR ATTRACTION
The Harapan Rain forest, a jungle reserve in Sumatra, Indonesia, is home to rhinoceros hornbills. These large birds have a unique habit—the female is imprisoned in a nest by a mud wall built by her mate, after she has laid eggs. The hornbill is the symbol of the Harapan reserve, and the state emblem of Sumatra. Conservationists often focus public attention on fascinating animals such as the hornbill and call them "flagship species." They devote lots of effort to saving flagship species, but their work usually benefits the whole ecosystem.

IF ENDANGERED ANIMALS are to survive in the wild, their natural habitats must be preserved and protected from damage. At the end of the 19th century, some governments began defending habitats by creating nature reserves, many of which they declared as national parks—set aside for people to enjoy nature. The world's first was at Yellowstone in the western United States. Its prairies and forests are home to rare timber wolves, lynx, and bison (as well as spectacular volcanic springs). In most nature reserves, mining, logging, hunting, fishing, and other ways of exploiting natural resources are banned. Reserves need rangers to enforce these bans and to control visitors. Some reserves, like Yellowstone, were created by forbidding anyone from living there, but some national parks have villages inside them. Balancing the needs of rare wildlife with the interests of human residents and visitors is all part of managing a national park.

CROWDED HOUSE
The largest of the world's 6,000 national parks is in Greenland and covers nearly 385,000 sq miles (1 million sq km)—larger than many countries! In creating a national park or nature reserve, authorities may fence off the area to prevent poachers or domestic animals from getting in and stop large wild mammals from leaving. In African savanna reserves, animals that could cause destruction to farms and villages are fenced in. But they can become overcrowded. Elephant herds may knock down all the trees, while grazing animals may strip the ground of food and drink all the available water. Park rangers sometimes need to manage their numbers by transferring them to other reserves, or even by killing some.

NOT JUST FOR DRAGONS

In 1980, a national park was set up to protect the Komodo dragon. This is the world's largest lizard species and it lives only on a few small islands in Indonesia. The Komodo National Park (KNP) covers the whole of Komodo Island and two smaller islands. That means the shallow sea between the islands is also part of the park. The KNP has become one of the best places in the world to see coral reefs and endangered marine species, such as whale sharks and ocean sunfish, as well as the monster lizards on land.

BEHIND BARBED WIRES

Wherever people are excluded, wildlife thrives. Nearly 60 years ago, a war between North Korea and South Korea ended, and both countries agreed to move their citizens out of a strip of land running between their borders. Since then, only animals have visited this demilitarized zone, or DMZ, including endangered species. Asiatic black bears have been hunted to extinction in Korea, except in the DMZ. Rare crane species also spend the winter there. Siberian tigers used to be found in Korea, and a few might survive in the untouched war zone.

WHALE ROUTES

In 2007, the route taken by giant cargo ships coming in and out of the port of Boston, Massachusetts, was changed after researchers found that endangered right whales used the same patch of water. In spring, half of the North Atlantic right whales in the world come to feed in the area, and many were killed by ships. Now, high-tech buoys in the water listen for the calls of whales and send warnings to ships that come too close to the animals.

Giraffes, zebras, and antelopes drink from a water hole in the Etosha National Park, Namibia, Africa

Gas-fueled chainsaw for trimming and cutting trees

MANAGING LANDSCAPES

Woodlands in parts of western Europe were once coppiced—people cut the trees near ground level for firewood. Coppiced trees regrew with many small trunks, which people harvested again. Many animals, such as nightingales and nightjars, do well in coppiced woodlands. So continuing the practice with modern tools such as chainsaws benefits wildlife. Park rangers manage reserves in other not-so-natural ways, such as controlling wetland water levels and providing nesting boxes for birds.

Chameleon's skin color resembles a dead leaf

PRICELESS REFUGE

Masaola National Park covers a peninsula in northeastern Madagascar. This single park is a refuge for an amazing array of rare animals. There are many types of lemur, including the endangered red ruffed species. An island within the reserve is home to the elusive aye-aye, while the park also contains the rare tomato frog, which releases a sticky substance from its skin when a predator tries to bite it. The park is also home to minute pygmy chameleons, some of the smallest reptiles that have ever lived.

Captive breeding

MONKEYING AROUND
Tamarins and marmosets are little monkeys that live in South America. Many of them are endangered because their forest habitat has been cut down. However, several species are now being saved by reintroduction programs. The monkeys breed easily in zoos—this captive white-headed marmoset is carrying her young. However, keepers have learned that monkeys that grow up in fixed cages are not safe up in trees in the wild—many fall to their deaths. Tamarins and marmosets being raised for reintroduction are now kept in trees so that they get used to the swaying branches.

PANDA PICNIC
These are the eight "Olympic pandas" picked by the people of China over the internet from among 16 giant pandas at the Wolong Panda Research Center, Sichuan Province. They were chosen to add cheer to the 2008 Beijing Olympics. There have been many attempts to breed the endangered giant panda in zoos, but with limited success, since captive pandas rarely mate. Recently, veterinarians have been using fertility treatment to make captive pandas pregnant, and their numbers are slowly going up. However, reintroducing the animals is also proving complicated. In 2006, a captive panda was released, but it survived only 10 months before dying in a fight with wild pandas.

IT IS TOO LATE TO SAVE SOME endangered animals in the wild. Their habitat is too damaged for them to survive there, so the only safe place for them is a zoo or wildlife park. But the species does not always have to stay behind a fence forever. Some species are being returned to the wild, a practice conservationists call reintroduction. Once an area of protected land has been prepared, the zoo animals are released into their natural habitat. However, experts are finding that reintroduction is not easy. Animals used to life in a zoo will not survive long on their own, so people must teach the animals how to live in the wild.

BORN TO BE WILD
Sometimes endangered animals are taken into captivity temporarily. Perhaps they need medical treatment or they are young animals that have lost their parents. This young lion grew up on a reserve in Namibia, Africa, and will some day be returned to the wild. The ranger is playing with it, as if it were a giant kitten. It is hoped that playing these games will teach the big cat how to behave with other lions one day when it joins a wild pride, or group.

OPERATION ORYX
The Arabian oryx is an antelope that once lived across the Middle East. It was almost driven to extinction by game hunters. However, before the last wild antelopes were shot in 1972, a few herds were taken to safety in zoos in Saudi Arabia and the US. One of the oldest captive breeding programs, Operation Oryx, was launched. Today, there are 6,000 Arabian oryxes, 1,000 of them living in the wild. All these animals were bred from a herd of barely 60 antelopes.

FOLLOWING THE LEADER
Many migratory birds are born not knowing where to fly in the fall when they migrate. The young ones follow their parents on the first flight and learn the route as they go. Birds that are reintroduced have to be shown the way by conservationists instead. Small microlight planes are used to lead young whooping cranes—one of North America's most threatened bird species—from Canada to the warmth of Florida in the fall. After that, the birds are able to find their way back on their own in spring.

Keeper hands a giant panda its favorite food, bamboo shoots

Dark-colored muzzle similar to that of the plains zebra

Stripes fade on rear haunches

BREEDING BACK THE DEAD
The quagga is an extinct type of zebra that lived in southern Africa. Quaggas had fewer stripes than other zebras and were thought to be a separate species. Genetic tests on preserved quagga skins, however, show that the quagga was a type of plains zebra, which is very much alive. In 1987, the Quagga Project began breeding quaggas from a herd of plains zebra. It has succeeded in breeding zebras that look similar to quaggas. However, few experts accept these animals are real quaggas returned from extinction.

18th-century illustration of a quagga

MOVING HOME
It is not always necessary to rescue a threatened species by removing it from the wild. In some cases, the species can be moved to a safe habitat. This practice is common in New Zealand, where some islands have never been invaded by damaging alien species. Island refuges are now the homes of all wild tuataras—a unique lizardlike reptile older than the dinosaurs—and all kakapos, too. The kakapo is a giant flightless parrot. There are just 124 of them left, but their tiny island homes appear to be safe, for now.

California condor

THE FACT THAT CONDORS CAN BE SEEN soaring above the mountains of southern California is a triumph of conservation. These scavenging birds scour the ground for dead animals. They once lived across the southwestern US, but suffered badly as people moved in. The birds were electrocuted by power lines and poisoned by lead bullets left in animals that had been shot. In 1937, the birds became extinct outside California. A small population survived in the hills above Los Angeles. But as that city grew, the birds continued to die out. By the mid-1980s, fewer than 10 wild birds were left. Was it too late for them?

Wingspan of 10 ft (3 m) is the largest among North American birds

PUPPET PARENTS
Condors were bred in zoos in the 1980s so that they could be reintroduced into the wild. When a female laid an egg, zookeepers took it away so she would soon lay another. When the eggs hatched, the zoo keepers raised the chicks by hand. However, they wanted the chicks to live as much like a wild bird as possible. The problem was solved using hand puppets. Keepers fed the condor chicks while wearing glove puppets that looked like their parents.

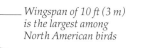

Antenna receives radio signals from tags on condors

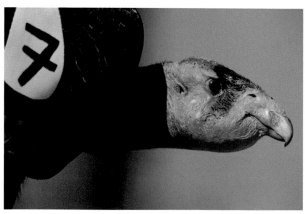

GROWING IN NUMBERS
In 1992, when the species had been extinct in the wild for seven years, conservationists released the first captive-born condors into the wild as part of the condor recovery program. Each reintroduced bird was tagged on the wings with a number so it could be identified from the ground as it flew. A total of 154 condors were released over the next decade. At first, the birds were freed into the mountains of California. Later, populations were set up around the Grand Canyon in Arizona and in Baja, Mexico. As of 2010, there are 322 California condors alive, with 172 of those in the wild.

RADIO TRACKING
Conservationists fitted released condors with radio tags. This equipment did not interfere with their flight, and it allowed scientists to follow the movements of different birds. This information was used to build up a picture of how the condors lived, and it helped conservationists locate the most suitable places to release other birds so they had a better chance of surviving in the wild. The radio tags also allow the team to track down and capture birds for regular blood tests and health checks before releasing them once again.

JUST IN TIME

People have known for a long time that California condors were disappearing. It was not until the 1980s that the US government decided the birds needed to be saved. By 1987, the entire species consisted of just 27 birds, all of them in zoos. Over the past 30 years, it has cost $100,000 per bird to build up today's population. However, the wild is still a dangerous place for condors. Their keepers try to frighten the birds every day—they hope this will teach the condors to stay away from people once they are released into the wild. This condor is soaring on an air current rising from high land.

Number on tag identifies condor

A California condor soaring over Yosemite's famous Half Dome

STATE SYMBOL

The California condor appeared on a quarter coin issued in 2005 to commemorate the founding of California in 1850. The bird is shown flying over Yosemite, California's first nature reserve. Also shown is John Muir, who helped found Yosemite and set up the Sierra Club, a conservation volunteer group.

HATCHING WILD

The condor rescue program has done a good job of getting condors back into the wild, but it will be for nothing if the zoo-born birds do not produce chicks of their own. The released condors began laying eggs in their rock-ledge nests, and in 2003, the first wild condor chick in recent times hatched. Most of the wild condors are too young to breed at present, so it is still early to tell if the wild population will increase.

TAKING FINGERPRINTS

Captive condors must not be allowed to breed with their close relatives, otherwise there are chances of genetic defects occurring. Scientists at California's San Diego Zoo produce genetic fingerprints of all the birds. These fingerprints show a bird's DNA (genetic material) as a series of bands. Closely related condors have fingerprints with very similar patterns of bands. The fingerprints help keepers mix the condors as much as possible, giving them the chance to produce healthy chicks.

Grassroots conservation

GOVERNMENTS MAY PROTECT endangered wildlife by creating nature reserves and national parks, but their conservation efforts could backfire if they ignore the needs of local people. To create the great game reserves of Kenya and Tanzania, locals, such as the Maasai, were excluded from their traditional grazing grounds. Excluded people may lose their livelihood, so it should be no surprise that poaching and habitat destruction still continue on the fringes of many nature reserves. If local people lose out due to wildlife conservation, they cannot be expected to cooperate. Since the 1980s, conservation efforts have moved to working with local communities. Local people themselves may also take action in what is called "grassroots conservation." The hope is that everyone will benefit from conservation and work together to save endangered animals.

WORKING WITH FARMERS

Jaguars are the largest cats in South America, and one of the fiercest predators. Ranchers dislike the cats because they sometimes kill their cattle. Many would shoot jaguars to protect their herds. However, a new conservation program in Brazil is working with farmers to protect the big cats. Farmers have learned that allowing other wildlife such as anteaters and deer onto the ranch gives the jaguars something else to prey on. Meanwhile, herds are kept moving around the farm and away from the forest, where jaguars might strike.

CHANGING SIDES

It may sound silly, but poachers make good gamekeepers—people who protect wild animals. Many poachers have been offered jobs in national parks as an alternative to breaking the law. Such ex-poachers are skilled at tracking rare animals and know where hunters are likely to strike. These game guards are using an elephant to patrol the Kaziranga National Park in Assam, India, home to the largest number of one-horned rhinoceroses in the world.

TRADITIONAL LIFESTYLES

Some groups of people have been living in rain forests for thousands of years without endangering any animals. But the traditional way of life of native people is under threat, just like the wildlife, as forests are cleared. In recent years, the native groups of some countries have won the right to take control of their lands. In many cases, native people choose to protect their land, including its habitats and wildlife. Davi Kopenawa Yanomami, shown here, is an activist from the Yanomami tribe in Brazil's Amazon rain forest. He has made people around the world aware of the problems facing tribal people in the Amazon region.

RESCUED BY RELIGION

Religions teach respect for all living things, and some religious institutions are centers for conservation. These Asian openbill storks live on the grounds of the Wat Phai Lom, a Buddhist temple on the outskirts of Bangkok, Thailand. Fifty years ago, the stork was rare in the country—the temple colony was the only group. Poachers threatened to wipe out this last flock, so in 1970 the temple was made a nature reserve. The birds came under the protection of the monks living there. Thanks to this refuge, openbills are now common and have formed new colonies across the region.

STARTING YOUNG

The conservation movement is still in its early days. People over the age of 40 grew up before environmental issues were taken seriously. Today, children are taught about ecology and conservation in school. These students are taking samples of river water to check for aquatic life and river pollution. It will teach them skills that could make them professional conservationists in the future.

MAKING IT PAY

Conservation can work by finding ways of making money by preserving a habitat. Instead of cutting down rain forests to grow coffee in fields, increasing numbers of farmers are creating forest plantations of shade-grown coffee. Coffee plants do not need bright sunlight and grow well under the shade of tall rain forest trees. The tall trees usually provide a fruit crop, and the plantation may harbor up to two-thirds of the bird species of natural rain forest. A forest plantation can also produce nuts, honey, and bananas, although because machines cannot get through the trees, it does require many workers to harvest the crops.

Shade-grown coffee beans

ECOTOURISM

A wildlife vacation is known as a safari—a term that comes from the Arabic word for travel. However, crowds of tourists can cause damage to what they came to see in the first place. For example, coral reefs are killed by tourists standing on them, and pollution from hotels can damage sensitive environments. Ecotourism aims to show tourists the wonders of nature without causing any of this damage—and the money it makes pays for conservation.

Friend-a-GORILLA

GORILLAS ONLINE

Conservation groups are using the internet to help save gorillas from extinction. The Friend-a-Gorilla campaign uses online social networks to find people to adopt an endangered mountain gorilla and donate money for its survival. Mountain gorillas are a highly endangered subspecies of the eastern gorilla and live in just a few patches of high, misty forest. If someone adopts a gorilla, they will soon be able to use their phone to track its family around their home in the Ugandan mountains. Wherever the person is in the world, they will know where their gorilla friend is.

Living with the relatives

THE NEED TO LOOK AFTER endangered animals is well understood today, but even so, conservationists do not always win. They face an almost impossible battle to protect gorillas. Gorillas are our close relatives, and among the most well-known of all African animals, but they still face a struggle for survival. The two living species are the western lowland gorilla and the eastern gorilla. There are fewer than 2,000 eastern gorillas living in the forests of eastern Democratic Republic of Congo, Rwanda, and Uganda. Although there are many more western lowland gorillas (an estimated 90,000), this species is equally at risk. Their forest habitat is under threat, and people even hunt them for food. It is not certain whether gorillas will survive.

STUDYING GORILLAS

Dian Fossey was an American scientist who lived alongside the mountain gorillas of Rwanda for 18 years. She learned how to communicate with the gorillas, so they would trust her and let her observe their behavior up close. Fossey became friends with some of the mountain gorillas, especially one she named Digit. When Digit was killed by poachers, Fossey arranged for armed guards to protect the gorillas. Fossey was murdered in 1985, but her work is still helping to protect the gorillas of Rwanda.

NO KING KONG

People often have the wrong idea about gorillas. The apes are not fierce creatures like King Kong, the giant gorilla that terrorizes people in movies. Gorillas are very big—the males are as tall as a man and weigh twice as much—but they eat leaves and fruits and are gentle by nature. Nevertheless, gorillas are immensely strong. Male gorillas give out signals to other gorillas by drumming their chests. This distinctive sound is also a warning that people should not get too close to them.

Model of a male gorilla at the American Museum of Natural History

LIFE IN A WAR ZONE

The eastern gorilla has the misfortune of living in a part of Africa where there have been long-lasting wars. Over the past 20 years, hundreds of thousands of people have been killed in fighting, especially in Rwanda and the Democratic Republic of Congo (Congo DR). Millions more have become refugees, forced to run away from their homes to find a safer place to live. Some refugees moved into the wildlife reserves along the borders of Rwanda and Congo DR, where 380 mountain gorillas—half of the entire subspecies—lived. Sadly, the new arrivals killed several of these gorillas.

HELP FROM TOURISTS
One of the best hopes for gorillas comes from tourism. Tour guides lead small groups of wildlife enthusiasts deep into the forests to see wild gorillas. The guides make sure the gorillas do not feel threatened. The local people are happy to help protect the gorillas because tourists bring jobs and money to the area. The Bwindi Impenetrable Forest in Uganda is one place with gorilla tours, and the idea seems to be working. Over the past decade, the number of gorillas there has risen.

GORILLA MEAT
Not everyone wants gorillas to live. Poachers still shoot the apes and sell their bodies for a high price. The heads and hands are sold as collectors' items, but most valuable is the gorilla meat. People do not eat gorilla meat just because they have no other food. Instead, they may buy it because it is so rare, and because meat from the wild, or bushmeat, is traditionally prized. Only the very rich can afford to serve gorilla meat to their guests. These four eastern gorillas were killed in the Congo rain forest, but poaching is a bigger threat to the western lowland gorillas, which are less protected.

DEADLY ENCOUNTERS
Among all animal species, the gorilla is one of the closest relatives of human beings. No one is quite sure if humans are nearest to them or to chimpanzees, but either way, there is not much difference—humans and gorillas share about 98 percent of their genes. Sadly, this close relationship is putting gorillas in great danger. The ebola virus causes a rare African disease that kills half of all the people it infects. It now appears to have spread to gorillas. They catch it from people or other animals that live along the edge of the forest. Loggers are clearing the forests where gorillas live, creating more chances of gorillas meeting people—and catching the virus.

The future

IT IS ALL TOO EASY for us to forget that we depend on the natural world for our survival. Water, food, fuel, and even the air, are all produced by a living system—or biosphere—on Earth. But that natural system is under pressure. We use twice as much fresh water today than we did in 1970, and many don't have enough. One-quarter of all land on Earth is used for farming, and more is being cleared. Do we need so much? In some seas, we have killed more than 90 percent of the fish that are caught for food. Can ocean life recover? Animals are now becoming extinct a thousand times faster than in the past thanks to humans, and that rate will rise further. We need to learn how to live by conserving Earth's natural resources. If we do not, we could soon be living in a world without most of the animals we know today. We may even make ourselves an endangered species.

PLANET OF PEOPLE
The number of humans is going up in some parts of the world, while in others it is staying roughly the same. The human population could stop growing at some point, but no one knows when. Earth's environment is struggling to support today's population. As poorer countries become richer, more pressure will be placed on Earth's resources. This will make saving endangered animals even harder.

Red List logo

Delete?

IN OUR HANDS
French artist Thierry Bisch is working with the IUCN to spread the message that humans can save endangered animals and build a way of life that does not damage the environment. He paints huge murals, or wall paintings, of endangered animals—like this black rhino. The artist has added a mouse cursor and a "Delete?" button. The painting tells us that we have the power to save wildlife and that we just have to decide to do it—or not.

SURVIVAL OF THE PRETTIEST
Conservation programs generally concentrate on endangered animals that appeal to people the most. We especially like species that share traits with us, such as gorillas and other apes, or impressive animals like tigers, elephants, and whales. We also choose to save animals that look the cutest, like this wide-eyed red panda. Smaller animals can get ignored—many people consider snakes too scary, insects too creepy, and shellfish just boring. However, whether we like these animals or not, ecosystems cannot work properly without all of them.

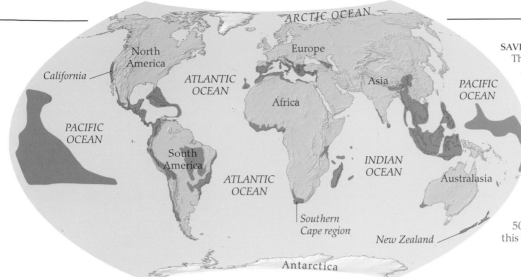

SAVING THE HOTSPOTS

The rate at which we are losing endangered animals means it will not be possible to save all of them. There is not enough time or money for conservation programs everywhere. So what should we save first? In 1988, British ecologist Norman Myers mapped "hotspots" where biodiversity—or the variety of life—was especially high. Scientists have identified 34 hotspots (shaded orange on the map), including Africa's southern Cape region, New Zealand, most of Southeast Asia, and parts of California. Incredibly, these hotspots cover less than 3 percent of Earth's land area, but contain 42 percent of all large animal species and 50 percent of all plant species. Myers argues that this is where conservation can be most effective.

Sunflower

CLEAN LIVING

Burning fossil fuels creates pollution, especially carbon dioxide. New car fuels such as biofuel could be much cleaner. Biofuel is made from sunflowers and other crops that take in carbon dioxide from the air as they grow. When biofuel burns, it releases the same carbon dioxide back into the air—so the amount of the gas always stays the same. Clean fuels could reduce the effects of climate change, but huge farms will be needed to grow crops for all the biofuel we require. This kind of clean energy might result in natural habitats being cleared and yet more animals becoming endangered.

WHOSE PLANET IS IT?

The 1968 film *Planet of the Apes* imagined a future Earth where humans have acted irresponsibly and destroyed their own civilization, probably in a nuclear war. Civilized apes have taken over as the ruling species and treat the few remaining humans as stupid animals, who they persecute as a nuisance. The story makes us think about whether we are really in charge of Earth. Are we treating the planet's resources and our fellow animals with enough respect?

A scene from the 2001 remake of *Planet of the Apes*

ANIMALS ON ICE

Some experts think that it will not be long before 10 large animal species become extinct every year. By the end of this century, one-eighth of all birds, one-quarter of all mammals, and one-third of all amphibians could have disappeared. One way to save them is to freeze the sperm and eggs of every species. These contain the genetic code, or genes, of each animal, and scientists place them in a store called a gene bank. Even if animals do become extinct in the future, it might be possible to use a gene bank to bring them back from the dead.

Researcher checks panda sperm stored in a liquid nitrogen container

Species at risk

ALTHOUGH MANY OF THE PROBLEMS facing animals today have been caused by our modern way of life, humans have had an impact on the natural world for a long time. Early humans would have witnessed many strange animals, such as giant kangaroos and cave lions, becoming extinct. People often caused these prehistoric extinctions, but climate change and diseases also played a part. Nevertheless, these ancient tragedies were completely natural. So when does an extinction become unnatural? Perhaps the answer is when we know an extinction is about to happen, but do nothing to stop it. Every endangered animal has its own unique story, and it is hard to keep track of them all, but we can see patterns among the many facts.

Introduced species

Habitat loss

Hunting

Others

ROUTES TO EXTINCTION
Humans have caused animal extinctions in three main ways: habitat destruction, hunting, and spreading pest animals from one continent to another. Often, it is a combination of all three factors that makes an animal extinct. This graphic shows causes of extinctions since 1600 CE. About one-quarter of these animals were hunted to extinction. One-third died out when their forests or other habitats were destroyed. Nearly 4 out of 10 extinctions were caused by animals from one part of the world being introduced to new regions.

Humans arrived in Australia around 40,000 years ago

Humans arrived in North America around 14,000 years ago

Humans arrived in Madagascar around 2,000 years ago

Survival of large mammal species (in percent)

100 80 60 40 20 0

100,000   10,000   1,000   100

Years ago

THE HUMAN EFFECT
The number of large mammal species drops drastically soon after humans arrive at a place for the first time. The main cause is probably hunting by humans, but in North America the climate was also changing and may have killed off many species. The first Australians might have seen giant wombats as big as rhinos and fierce marsupial lions. In America, early humans lived alongside tall dire wolves and giant sloths. The number of mammals in Madagascar also fell, but has gone up in recent centuries as people have introduced farm animals and pest species.

RED FOR DANGER
It is a sad fact that the more experts learn about biodiversity, the more endangered animals they discover. The scientists behind the IUCN's Red List have a lot of work to do checking all the species known, and new ones are being found all the time. The graphic below shows the main vertebrate animal groups. The red sections indicate the proportion of these species that are under threat. However, the scientists have only a dim view of the true size of the problem. Only about 1 in 10 of fish and reptile species have been checked so far.

REPTILES
Species evaluated = 1,677
Threatened species = 469

FISH
Species evaluated = 4,443
Threatened species = 1,414

MAMMALS
Species evaluated = 5,490
Threatened species = 1,142

AMPHIBIANS
Species evaluated = 6,285
Threatened species = 1,895

A WORLD VIEW

This map shows how many endangered animals live in each continent. Many of these animals live in more than one continent, so adding up all the totals would exceed the actual overall number. The map tells us that Asia, the largest continent, has the most endangered animals. However, why does Oceania—the smallest region—have so many? It could be because Oceania has thousands of islands that dot the Pacific Ocean, and many of them are home to threatened species. The continent with the fewest listed species is Antarctica, because very few animals live there at all. However, Oceania seems to have more than South America, which is home to the richest rain forest on Earth. However, we still do not know enough about what lives in South America to count all of its endangered animals.

NORTH AMERICA 3,626 species

EUROPE 1,978 species

ASIA 7,067 species

AFRICA 4,902 species

SOUTH AMERICA 2,280 species

OCEANIA 3,187 species

ANTARCTICA 50 species

LOSING FORESTS

Since the end of the last ice age, humans have cut down almost half of the forests on Earth. It took people 8,000 years to clear one-third of the forests—mostly the trees covering Europe and Asia. About 14 percent disappeared in the last 150 years alone. Roughly two-thirds of the remaining woodland is secondary forest—regrown after felling by loggers or by people cutting firewood. Only one-fifth of Earth's original wooded land remains as untouched primary forest. Most recently, tropical rain forests, where most of Earth's species live, have been felled. Clearing rain forests has made thousands of animals endangered.

47% of Earth's forest cover lost over past 8,000 years

31% of the remaining forest is secondary forest

22% of primary forest now survives

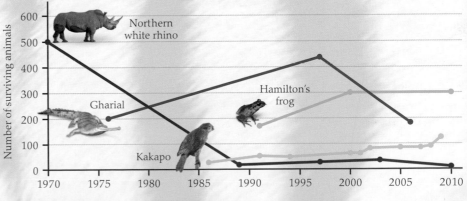

KEEPING TRACK

This graph shows the mixed fortunes of four critically endangered animals. While the southern white rhino was protected from poachers, the northern subspecies in the Congo region became extinct in the wild in 2010. The gharial was given a boost by captive breeding in the 1980s, but the wild populations have not thrived. The kakapo used to be one of the rarest birds on Earth until it was relocated to safe islands in New Zealand. The number of Hamilton's frog almost doubled in 10 years because it too has been moved by conservationists to islands off New Zealand that are free of rats.

BIRDS
Species evaluated = 9,998
Threatened species = 1,223

65

Timeline

FOSSIL EXPERTS have measured how often animals become extinct. In the 65 million years since the last mass extinction that wiped out the dinosaurs, just one-tenth of 1 percent of mammal species became extinct every 1,000 years—the natural rate of extinction. Today, extinctions are more common due to human activities, with the same number of mammals dying out every 10 years. This timeline shows the most important extinctions since the dinosaurs disappeared.

Woolly rhino

Gastornis

65 MYA END OF THE DINOSAURS
Dinosaurs and many other large reptiles die out.

60 MYA SNAKES AND LIZARDS
Surviving reptiles such as snakes and lizards are among the first species to take the place of dinosaurs. One of the largest is a giant snake, *Titanoboa*, which grew up to 43 ft (13 m) long.

45 MYA *GASTORNIS*
Gastornis, a huge, flightless hunting bird standing 6½ ft (2 m) tall, becomes extinct.

35 MYA GIANT PREDATOR
Andrewsarchus, one of the largest land predators ever, becomes extinct. This giant hunter was a relative of today's hoofed animals. Scientists think it weighed up to 2,200 lb (1,000 kg) and lived on grasslands in Asia.

34 MYA THUNDER BEASTS
The brontotheres (or "thunder beasts") become extinct. These giant grazers had a huge Y-shaped horn growing from the snout.

25 MYA LARGEST MAMMALS
Paraceratherium, the largest mammal ever to walk the Earth, becomes extinct. Standing 16 ft (5 m) at its shoulder, *Paraceratherium* would have towered over today's elephants.

10 MYA CHALK BEAST
The unusual *Chalicotherium* (or "chalk beast") becomes extinct. It had long forelegs and large claws, which made walking difficult, but allowed it to pull down branches and leaves from trees.

3 MYA HUMAN ANCESTOR
Australopithecus, an early human ancestor, becomes extinct. The most complete *Australopithecus* fossil found was called "Lucy." Its bones told us these ancestors of ours were just 4 ft 4 in (1.3 m) tall.

2 MYA TERRORBIRD
The terrorbird was the nickname for several giant birds that evolved after the dinosaurs died out. One of the fiercest was *Titanis*, which hunted in the Americas until about 2 million years ago. It was flightless, stood 10 ft (3 m) tall, and had a huge crushing beak.

1.6 MYA MEGA SHARK
The largest hunting shark, *Megalodon*, becomes extinct. This fish was at least 53 ft (16 m) long and had a mouth 6½ ft (2 m) wide. A grown man could stand inside its mouth.

40,000 YA AUSTRALIAN MONSTERS
Two giant species in Australia become extinct. *Diprotodon* was a huge grazing marsupial the size of a modern rhino and a relative of today's koalas. *Megalania* was one of the largest lizard species ever, growing up to 23 ft (7 m) long. Both these extinctions occurred around the time humans arrived in Australia.

37–26,000 YA NEANDERTHALS
The Neanderthal, a species of human that lived in Europe and the Middle East during the last ice age, becomes extinct as it is replaced by the modern human species spreading from Africa.

10,000 BCE LAST HUMAN EXTINCTION
Flores Man could be the last human species to become extinct. Some believe the 3-ft- (1-m-) tall humans that lived on the Indonesian island of Flores belonged to a separate species of human.

9,000 BCE SABER-TOOTHED CAT
Smilodon, a saber-toothed cat, becomes extinct as open grasslands are slowly replaced by forests and its prey of grazing animals dies out.

8,000 BCE WARMING WORLD
Several large animals die out in the Americas as the world warms out of the last ice age and humans spread across the land. They include *Megatherium*, a 5½-ton (5-metric-ton) ground sloth. In Asia, the woolly rhino also dies out.

7,500 BCE IRISH ELK
The Irish elk, a giant deer, becomes extinct. Its antlers grew to more than 11½ ft (3.5 m) across. The species lived across Europe and Asia.

1,700 BCE WOOLLY MAMMOTHS
The last of the woolly mammoths becomes extinct on Wrangel Island in the Arctic Ocean.

300s BCE LADDER OF LIFE
The Greek philosopher Aristotle becomes one of the first to classify animals. He believed animals were positioned on a "ladder of life," with humans at the top and simple animals lower down on it.

1000–1500s CE GIANT FOSSA
The giant fossa, a 6½-ft- (2-m-) long predator of lemurs and elephant birds, becomes extinct on Madagascar. The extinction may have happened due to the loss of large koala lemurs, a species of lemur, at the same time.

Megalania

MYA: MILLION YEARS AGO
YA: YEARS AGO
BCE: BEFORE COMMON ERA
CE: COMMON ERA

1400s GIANT MOAS
Giant moas become extinct in New Zealand following the arrival of Māori settlers. The Māori hunted the large birds for food and also introduced the first rats and dogs to the land.

1500s CUBAN CONEY
The Cuban coney, a rodent living in Cuba and related to guinea pigs, is one of the first extinctions brought about by European settlers.

1627 AUROCHS
The aurochs, the wild ancestor of domestic cattle, becomes extinct. Aurochs once lived in Europe, North Africa, and southern Asia. The last recorded sighting was of a female in Poland.

1650s ELEPHANT BIRDS
The last elephant birds are sighted in Madagascar. Elephant birds were colossal, weighing as much as three ostriches. Their eggs were 15 times larger than an ostrich egg, today's largest.

Aristotle

1681 DODO
The dodo, a giant relative of pigeons, and living on the island of Mauritius, becomes extinct about a 100 years after being discovered. The island had no large predators and the dodos had no ability to protect themselves from humans.

1700 NIGHT HERON
The Réunion night heron was first described by a biologist in 1674, but it appears to have disappeared from Réunion Island in the Indian Ocean by the start of the 18th century.

1768 SEA COW
Steller's sea cow, a relative of today's manatees and dugongs, becomes extinct due to hunting, just 27 years after it is discovered.

1796 GEORGES CUVIER
The French naturalist Georges Cuvier proves from his research into fossils of mammoths and woolly rhinos that animal species can become extinct and disappear.

1800s MĀORI DOG
The Māori dog, or kuri, becomes extinct.

1850 BLUE ANTELOPE
The bluebuck, or blue antelope, is the first large African species to disappear in modern times.

1852 GREAT AUK
The great auk, a fish-eating flightless Atlantic seabird, is hunted to extinction.

1866 NATURAL HISTORY MUSEUM
The Natural History Museum opens in London, UK, and starts putting together one of the greatest collections of animal specimens in the world.

1870 ATLAS BEAR
The Atlas bear, a subspecies of the brown bear that lived in the mountains of North Africa, is spotted for the last time.

1872 FIRST NATIONAL PARK
Yellowstone in the US is declared the world's first national park.

1875 NEW ZEALAND QUAIL
The New Zealand quail, known as the koreke by the Māori, becomes extinct a little more than 100 years after first being described.

1876 FALKLAND ISLAND WOLF
The Falkland Island wolf is hunted to extinction. It is the first dog species to be made extinct in human history.

1883 QUAGGA
The quagga, a zebra subspecies from southern Africa, becomes extinct after the last living specimen dies in Amsterdam Zoo.

1889 RSPB
The Society for the Protection of Birds—today's RSPB—is formed in Britain to fight against the use of rare bird feathers in women's hats. The society was allowed to add the "Royal" to its name in 1904.

1890 WILD HORSE
The European wild horse, or tarpan, becomes extinct in the wild.

1904 CAROLINA PARAKEET
The Carolina parakeet becomes extinct in the wild. Fourteen years later the last captive animal dies. The Carolina parakeet was the only native parrot species in the eastern United States.

1914 LAUGHING OWL
The last whekau, or laughing owl, is seen in South Island, New Zealand. The hunting bird made many strange noises, from chuckles and shrieks to whistles and hoots, which some people heard as late as the 1960s.

Steller's sea cow

1929 EELGRASS LIMPETS
A disease of eelgrass kills off the eelgrass limpet, a sea snail living along the east coast of Canada and New England.

1930 GALÁPAGOS MOUSE
Darwin's Galápagos mouse becomes extinct after first being found in 1906, due to mice and rats introduced from the mainland.

1936 TASMANIAN TIGER
The thylacine, also known as the Tasmanian tiger and Tasmanian wolf, becomes extinct when the last specimen dies in Hobart Zoo. The species had become extinct in the wild six years before.

1938 SCHOMBURGK'S DEER
The last known captive specimen of Schomburgk's deer dies. In 1932, the last known wild deer of this species was shot by a hunter in Thailand.

1940 HAWAIIAN FINCH
The Hawaii akialoa, a sickle-billed finch, becomes the next Hawaiian bird to become extinct as its forest habitat is cleared away.

1941 XERXES BUTTERFLY
The Xerxes blue butterfly becomes extinct as the city of San Francisco in California expands over the species' habitat—sand dunes along the Pacific coast. It is one of the first American species to die out due to urban expansion.

Xerxes blue butterfly

1942 BARBARY LION
The North African subspecies of the lion becomes extinct in the wild. These lions had longer manes than other subspecies. Barbary lions were kept in captivity since Roman times.

1943 DESERT BANDICOOT
The desert bandicoot, a marsupial with a lifestyle similar to a raccoon, is sighted for the last time in its dry habitat in central Australia.

1948 IUCN
The International Union for Conservation of Nature, or IUCN, is founded at Fontainebleau, France, with its headquarters beside Lake Geneva in Switzerland.

1951 YEMENI GAZELLE
The last sighting of the Queen of Sheba's gazelle is made in the mountains of Yemen. This extinction is one of the most recent large mammal species to be lost due to human activity.

1952 MONK SEAL
The Caribbean monk seal becomes the first seal species to be made extinct. It had been hunted since the 1500s for its skin, oil, and meat.

1958 CASPIAN TIGER
The west Asian subspecies of the tiger becomes extinct. It once lived in the mountains of Iran, central Asia, and even Georgia and Turkey.

1961 WWF
The World Wildlife Fund, or WWF, charity is founded in Switzerland. Later renamed the World Wide Fund for Nature, it becomes the largest conservation organization in the world.

Przewalski's horse

1962 SILENT SPRING
Rachel Carson publishes *Silent Spring*, a book that introduced the public to the dangers of environmental damage caused by pollution.

1968 FLYING FOX
The last Guam flying fox, a small fruit bat, is shot by a hunter. Habitat destruction on its Pacific island home led to its decline.

1975 CITES
The Convention on International Trade in Endangered Species of Wild Fauna and Flora (CITES) is agreed upon by members of the IUCN.

1982 OPERATION ORYX
Operation Oryx releases the first captive-bred Arabian oryx into a reserve in Oman, after the animal became extinct in the wild in 1972.

1985 CHRISTMAS ISLAND SHREW
After last being seen in 1958, two Christmas Island shrews are captured. However, the captive specimens soon die, and no member of the species has been seen since.

1985 PRZEWALSKI'S HORSE
Conservationists reintroduce 11 Przewalski's horses to the steppes of northwest China, and the horses begin breeding well. Przewalski's horse had survived in captivity after becoming extinct in the wild in 1966.

1986 SAVING THE WHALES
The International Whaling Commission's ban on hunting whales comes into force. Only a handful of large whales are allowed to be killed each year for scientific purposes, although their meat is often still sold as food.

1987 KAUAI OO
The calls of the Kauai oo, a Hawaiian bird, are recorded for the final time.

1990 NEW ZEALAND BAT
The New Zealand greater short-tailed bat is feared extinct after not being seen since 1967. The bat was one of only three land-based mammal species (all bats) native to New Zealand.

1992 EARTH SUMMIT
The Earth Summit is held in Rio de Janeiro, Brazil, with representatives of 172 countries meeting to discuss environmental issues. One of the agreements made was the Convention on Climate Change to tackle global warming.

1995 ST. HELENA EARWIG
Remains of a Saint Helena earwig—at 3 in (80 mm) long, the largest earwig in the world—are found on the remote Atlantic island. No live earwig has been seen since 1967, but the species is still thought to survive.

1996 ROUND ISLAND BOA
The Round Island burrowing boa, one of two species of boa living on the Indian Ocean island, is declared extinct.

1996 LAS VEGAS FROG
The Vegas Valley leopard frog is declared extinct after the spring-fed streams it lived in dry out as water is diverted to the growing city of Las Vegas.

1997 KYOTO PROTOCOL
At the third meeting of the United Nations' Convention on Climate Change in Kyoto, Japan, the Kyoto Protocol is agreed to by most of the world's countries that seek to reduce the amount of carbon dioxide they release.

Golden toad

2002 GASTRIC-BROODING FROGS
Both species of gastric-brooding frogs of Australia are classified as extinct.

2003 SEYCHELLES BLACK TERRAPIN
The Seychelles black terrapin is declared extinct after searches in 1996 fail to find any of the turtlelike animals on the Indian Ocean islands.

2004 YUNNAN BOX TURTLE
A Yunnan box turtle is found in a pet store in China. The species was declared extinct in 2000, but then reclassified as critically endangered.

2005 MEXICAN PORPOISE
An ocean reserve is set up in the Gulf of California to protect the last 400 vaquitas, a porpoise unique to that narrow seaway. However, trawler fishing is still allowed in the area, and by 2009 the vaquita population had fallen to 150 after many were caught in nets. In 2010, trawling was finally banned.

2006 REINTRODUCED PANDA
A zoo-bred giant panda is released to live in the wild for the first time. However, the animal dies in 2007 after a fight with wild pandas.

2008 GOLDEN TOAD
The golden toad of Costa Rica is declared extinct after not being seen since 1989. Causes of the extinction include the chytrid fungus, and the shrinking size of the toad's' cool mountain forest.

2009 PYRENEAN IBEX
The extinct Pyrenean subspecies of the Iberian ibex is cloned from skin samples, only to die shortly after birth.

2010 IVORY DATING
A test is introduced to check whether ivory objects are made from new or old ivory. Selling fresh ivory is illegal, but objects made from antique ivory are still allowed.

Tail of a blue whale

Find out more

YOU CAN MEET endangered animals at your nearest zoo or in the wild—in your local nature reserve, for instance. You could even join the fight to protect them. Find out about wildlife reserves in your neighborhood using the internet or at the library. Wardens or rangers at the reserve can tell you about the rare animals living there. They may also help you get involved with local conservation volunteers. Good zoos provide facts about their animals and may be conducting conservation breeding programs. Ask them if they need volunteers. Finally, you could contact an international conservation organization and join in raising awareness and funds for the protection of endangered species.

GARDEN OF LIFE
You can make your own patch of wilderness by planting a flower garden at home or at school. The garden will be a haven for butterflies, beetles, and other insects. These in turn will provide food to larger animals such as wild birds, hedgehogs, and toads. A good insect garden needs a mix of different flowers and should be allowed to get messy, since a tangle of plants will provide even more shelter for animals.

BECOMING A CONSERVATIONIST
There are endangered animals everywhere—even in your neighborhood—and you can help them. Local conservation groups work to clean up wild places and make it easier for people to visit them. They also record the different wildlife coming in to and out of an area each year. Many of these groups will have activities suitable for all ages. These local cub scouts and brownies are collecting starfish from the seabed off Hong Kong. The starfish will be transplanted to another bay where pollution had killed all sea life, but which was later cleaned up and made suitable for animals.

Places to visit

SAN DIEGO ZOO, SAN DIEGO, CALIFORNIA
One of the largest zoos in the world, the San Diego Zoo is a leader in the captive breeding of endangered animals. The imaginative enclosures offer a chance to see animals behaving like they would in the wild.
- The zoo contains 800 species from all over the world. Endangered species include pandas, bonobos, and black rhinos.
- Larger animals like African elephants and giraffes are kept at the zoo's separate Wild Animal Park.

EVERGLADES NATIONAL PARK, FLORIDA
Although there are 58 national parks in the United States, this is one of the largest and protects an amazing wetland habitat.
- There are dozens of endangered animals living in the park, including leatherback sea turtles, American crocodiles, Florida panthers, and manatees.
- Park activities include hiking, canoeing, fishing, and wilderness camping.

NATIONAL ZOO, WASHINGTON, D.C.
The Smithsonian's National Zoo is a free, 163-acre zoological park in the heart of the nation's capital.
- The park's most popular animals are the giant pandas, Tian Tian and Mei Xiang. The pair is due to return to China in December 2010, but their fans hope the zoo will negotiate an extended stay.
- The zoo also operates a conversation and research center in nearby Front Royal, Virginia, which is closed to the public.

AMERICAN MUSEUM OF NATURAL HISTORY, NEW YORK, NEW YORK
Filled with incredible specimens and lifelike models, the AMNH is a great place to learn about the biodiversity of animal life, from prehistoric times to the present.
- The Milstein Hall of Ocean Life features an incredible life-size model of a blue whale, 94 ft (29 m) in length.
- The Hall of Biodiversity includes 1,500 specimens of living things, as well as a simulated rain-forest environment.

USEFUL WEBSITES

- The website of the IUCN Red List provides details of threats faced by endangered species: **www.iucnredlist.org**
- The ARKive website is a collection of photos and video clips of endangered animals from around the world: **www.arkive.org**
- The website for the World Wide Fund for Nature, previously known as the World Wildlife Fund, provides details of the many conservation programs run by the organization: **www.wwf.org**
- The website of the Smithsonian National Zoo has many animal facts and conservation information: **www.nationalzoo.si.edu**
- Animal Planet's site features photos and facts about a wide range of endangered species: **www.animal.discovery.com/guides/endangered/endangered.html**

Glossary

Living fossil:
an aardvark

AMPHIBIAN
A class of animal that includes frogs, toads, newts, and salamanders. Most amphibians begin life in water, but spend their adult lives on land.

ATMOSPHERE
A mixture of gases that surrounds a planet. Earth's atmosphere contains oxygen and carbon dioxide (two gases used by living things) and nitrogen.

BIODIVERSITY
The variety of living things. Some areas of the world have greater biodiversity than others.

BIOFUEL
A gaslike fuel made from certain crops. When biofuel is burned it releases steam and carbon dioxide into the air. The carbon dioxide is taken out of the air by more biofuel crops as they grow, so the amount of carbon dioxide in the air stays the same no matter how much biofuel is burned.

Biome: a temperate rain forest

BIOME
A living community with distinctive plant and animal species developed in the specific conditions of a particular region. Temperate rain forest, desert, and coral reef are all examples of biomes.

BIOSPHERE
The area of Earth in which life exists. It extends several miles up into the atmosphere, down to the bottom of the oceans, and even into the rocks of Earth's crust.

CLIMATE CHANGE
The way Earth's weather patterns change over long periods, so regions of the planet that were once cold and dry become warm and wet. Changes to the climate are now being caused by humans putting carbon dioxide and other gases into the air, mostly due to burning forests and fuels.

CLONE
An animal that shares its DNA (genetic material) with another animal. Identical twins are natural clones, but scientists can also create cloned animals in the laboratory.

CONSERVATION
Working to save habitats and endangered wildlife.

DNA
The short form for deoxyribonucleic acid, the chemical that carries the genetic code in all animals and most other living things.

ECOLOGY
The study of how animals, plants, and other living things interact with each other and with their environment.

ECOSYSTEM
The name given to a wildlife community that survives in a particular habitat.

ECOTOURISM
A wildlife vacation that aims to have a minimum impact on the environment. Its charges are used to pay for conservation.

EVOLUTION
Describes how living things change slowly over many generations by the process of natural selection (see NATURAL SELECTION). Animals adapt to changes in the environment by evolving.

EXOTIC
From a foreign country, the opposite of native. Exotic animals often make native animals endangered, especially on islands.

EXTINCT
An animal becomes extinct when all the members of its species have died out. Extinctions may be natural or caused by humans.

FERTILIZER
A substance added to soil to help crops grow quickly. Natural fertilizers include feces and rotting material. Artificial fertilizers are made from nitrogen gas taken from the air.

FOOD CHAIN
A way of describing what the wildlife in an ecosystem eats. Each link in the chain shows one animal (or plant) that is eaten by another. The chain continues to the top predator or the animal that has no natural enemies.

FOSSIL
The remains or other evidence of an ancient living thing that has been preserved as stone. Most fossils are made from hard bones.

Keystone species: a leather starfish preys
on mussels and balances an ecosystem

FOSSIL FUELS
The name for gas, natural gas, and coal, which are natural fuels that developed from the buried remains of forests and sea life over millions of years.

FUNGI
A group of living things that are neither animals nor plants. Familiar fungi are mushrooms, molds, and yeast.

GENE BANK
A store of frozen sperm, eggs, or seeds, all containing the genetic instructions, or genes, that are kept in case a species becomes extinct or cannot reproduce naturally.

GENETICS
The science that seeks to understand how genes—the coded instructions in DNA—lead to living things growing and developing the way they do.

GENUS
A group of closely related species that are thought to have evolved from a recent common ancestor.

HABITAT
The environment of an animal or plant or any other living thing.

HOTSPOT
Biodiversity hotspots are regions of Earth with a rich concentration of different plants and animals.

INVERTEBRATE ANIMALS
Animals that do not have a backbone, such as insects, worms, and starfish.

IRRIGATION
Diverting water from natural sources to crops that do not receive enough rain to grow naturally.

KEYSTONE SPECIES
An important member of an ecosystem that forms a crucial link between the other wildlife. If a keystone species becomes endangered then other animals in the ecosystem will also struggle.

LIVING FOSSIL
A species that has not changed much in appearance for millions of years and still looks like its ancient relatives. The aardvark (above) has changed little since it developed several millions of years ago.

MAMMAL
A class of animal that includes sheep, tigers, whales, and humans. Unlike any other type of animal, all mammals have at least some hair and feed their babies with milk.

Migration:
Eurasian curlews

MASS EXTINCTION
A large number of species becoming extinct in a short time due to drastic environmental change.

METEORITE
The remains of a rock from space, or asteroid, that has traveled through Earth's atmosphere and smashed into it. Large asteroids cause huge disasters that can kill much of the life on Earth.

MIGRATION
A regular journey made by animals to find places to feed, mate, or raise their young. Most migrations are two-way journeys, the outward part in spring followed by the return leg in the fall.

Mollusk: a snail

MOLLUSK
A huge class of invertebrate animals, many of which have shells. Mollusks include snails, slugs, mussels, and squid.

NATIVE
Refers to the region or country of origin of a species. The animal is said to be native to that place. Native animals are often endangered by species introduced from elsewhere.

NATURALIST
Someone who is an expert in wildlife after studying animals in the wild.

NATURAL SELECTION
The process by which living things that are poorly suited to life in their environment are gradually killed off by natural causes. Their relatives that are better suited to their environment are more likely to survive.

NATURAL RESOURCES
The materials people collect from the Earth. Important natural resources are water, metals, fuel, food, wood, and stone.

NICHE
The place a species holds in an ecosystem, including where it lives, how it finds food, and which other species it comes into contact with.

NOCTURNAL
To be active at night. Nocturnal animals may have sensitive eyesight, but they also use their senses of smell, hearing, and touch to find what they need in the dark.

NUTRIENTS
Substances needed by living things for growth or energy, including sugars, proteins, fats, vitamins, and elements such as iron and nitrogen.

PARASITE
An organism that lives on or inside another, known as a host, and harms it. Parasitic animals include fleas, lice, and tapeworms.

PESTICIDE
A chemical that is used to poison pests, normally insects, that attack crops and infest homes. The chemical is often not deadly to nonpest animals, but may cause health problems if used wrongly.

PLANKTON
Living things that cannot control where they move and instead float in water—and sometimes in the air. Most plankton are tiny plants, animals, and microorganisms.

POACHER
A person who hunts animals that are protected by the law or belong to someone else.

POLLUTION
Anything that has been added to the environment by people that then causes problems, such as killing plants and animals, or making people unwell.

POPULATION
The total number of a particular group of animal of one species.

PREDATOR
An animal that hunts and kills other animals for its food.

PREHISTORIC
Describes the time before people began to record events in history.

RAIN FOREST
A type of forest that grows in areas where it rains a lot all year round.

REPTILE
A class of animal—including lizards, snakes, turtles, and crocodiles—whose members have dry, scaly skin.

SPECIES
A population of animals whose members look very similar, live in the same kind of way, and can breed with each other.

SPECIMEN
Something taken from the wild as an example to show other people.

SPERM
A type of cell produced by male animals, fungi, and most plants, that carries genes. Sperm combines with an egg from a female to produce a baby animal or new plant.

STONE AGES
Periods in early human history when people used stone as their main construction material, making weapons and tools with it.

SUBSPECIES
A population of animals of a certain species that lives in a particular part of the world. For example, the tiger species is divided into nine subspecies. Members of a subspecies look slightly different from animals in another.

TAXONOMY
The practice of identifying, naming, and classifying species, based on how they look, or on their DNA, and on how they seem to be related.

VIRUS
A disease-causing agent made of DNA and protein. The virus invades the bodies of living things and uses them to copy itself and increase its number. As it does this, the animal or plant may become sick or even die.

WILDERNESS
An area that has not been significantly affected by humans and remains completely wild.

Reptile:
a San Francisco
garter snake

Index

Acknowledgments

Dorling Kindersley would like to thank:
Charlotte Webb for proofreading and Monica Byles for the index.

The Publishers would like to thank the following for their kind permission to reproduce their photographs:

(Key: a-above; b/b-background; b-below/bottom; bl-below left; br-below right; c-center; cl-center left; cr-center right; l-left; r-right; t-top; tl-top left; tr-top right; crb-center right below; cra-center right above.)

Alamy Images: Derrick Alderman 35cr; Peter Arnold, Inc 23br, 56br; Peter Arnold, Inc. 41tr; Blickwinkel 37cr; Bronstein 32–33b; John Cancalosi 3b, 56–57; Coinery 4clb, 57cr; Custom Life Science Images, Inc; Enigma 4bc, 4bc; John T. Fowler 67br; Bob Gibbons 30cl; Mark Goble 41c; imagebroker 8cl, 62t; Juniors Bildarchiv 30–31; Wolfgang Kaehler 28c; Frans Lemmens 45tr; LOOK Die Bildagentur der Fotografen GmbH 36bl; The Natural History Museum 2tc, 4cra, 9cr, 13br; Rolf Nussbaumer Photography 31br; Michael Patrick O'Neill 12b, 33cb; Photoshot Holdings Ltd 29tl; Pictorial Press Ltd 47tr; Vova Pomortzeff 21br; Robert Harding Picture Library Ltd 45bl; Clive Sawyer 33tr; John Sullivan 71br; Jeremy Sutton-Hibbert 2tr, 44–45, 51cr; Duncan Usher 62–63; **Ardea:** Nick Gordon 34cl; Joanna Van Gruisen 43tl; Ken Lucas 39cr; Pat Morris 28tr; Kenneth W.Fink 6tl;

Biodiversity Institute of Ontario/Suz Bateson: 9crb; **Corbis:** 56tr; James L. Amos 68l; Atlantide Phototravel 27t; Bettmann, 8–9; Tom Brakefield, 1, 17cl; Ralph A. Clevenger 16bl; Howard Davies 60b; Nigel Dennis; Gallo Images 54c; Eric Draper/Aurora Photos 37tr; How Hwee Young/epa 14tl; Kevin Fleming 19cr; Frank Lane Picture Agency 45tl; The Gallery Collection 7cr; David T. Grewcock/Frank Lane Picture Agency 49ca; Louise Gubb 58–59b; Martin Harvey 52–53b, 61tr; Chris Hellier, 6bl; Andrew Holbrooke, 50–51; Hulton-Deutsch Collection 11tr; Frans Lanting 2crb, 41tl, 42tl; Frederic Larson/San Francisco Chronicle 43b; John Lee/Aurora Photos 6clb; Joe McDonald 14bl; Amos Nachoum 16cr; Michael Nicholson 50cl; Radius Images 14–15b; Hans Reinhard 40c; Lynda Richardson 38b; Jeffrey L. Rotman 19tr, 46–47; Sanford/Agliolo 25tl; Kevin Schafer 24tl, 24–25; Michael St. Maur Sheil 41br; Paul Souders 4tl, 38–39; Keren Su 11tl; Jeff Vanuga 29br; Visuals Unlimited 39r; Kennan Ward 18tl, 42cl; Stuart Westmorland 70b; Ronald Wittek/dpa 54tl; Luo Xiaoguang/Xinhua Press 54–55; **Detroit Public Library/Burton Historical Collection:** 44bl; **Dorling Kindersley:** Geoff Brightling, Courtesy of University College, London 26fcl; Geoff Brightling/ESPL-modelmaker (c) ESPL 26r; Courtesy of the Pitt Rivers Museum, University of Oxford 27c; Frank Greenaway, Courtesy of the National Birds of Prey Center, Gloucestershire, 13fcl; Jon Hughes 25tr; Colin Keates 24cl, 24fcl; Colin Keates, Courtesy of the Natural History Museum, London 3tl, 17cr, 24cr, 26cl; Courtesy of the Linnean Society of London 8br; Gary Ombler, Courtesy of Paradise Park, Cornwall 65b; Harry Taylor, Courtesy of the Natural

History Museum, London 67tr; Kim Taylor 7tr; friendagorilla.org: 60tl; **Getty Images:** 9tr, 46bl, 51br; AFP 8bl, 15tl, 29tr, 37br, 49tr, 51tl, 63br, 69b; Tom Brakefield 58tc; Brandon Cole 46tl; Max Dannenbaum 33ca; Dinodia Photos 7l; David Doubilet 6cla; Paul E.Tessier 35t; Gerry Ellis 34r; Don Farrall 13cl; Sue Flood 35bl; Michael Fogden 68tr; Jeff Foott 65bl; Fotog crb, 28–29b; Martin Harvey, 13cr; Wim van den Heever 64crb; Richard Hermann/Visuals Unlimited, Inc. 68b; Andrew Holt 29ca; Jeff Hunter, 16–17t; Robb Kendrick 43tr; Frans Lemmens 64cr; George Loun 59c; Joe McDonald 7br, 53tr; Mason Morfit 27br; National Geographic 56bl; Stan Osolinski 55tl; Martin Ruegner 15br; Joel Sartore 21tr, 64–65br; Kevin Schafer 53br; Anup Shah 48cl; SSPL 11bl; SuperStock 61cr; Tetra Images 4cla, 29cl; Ron and Patty Thomas 70l; Tony Tilford 8cr; Ann & Steve Toon 58tl; Greg Vaughn 2br, 33br; Sven Zacek 29cr; **IUCN (International Union for Conservation of Nature):** 16cl; Chris Jordan: 42cr; **The Kobal Collection:** Sam Emerson/ 20th Century/Zanuck Co. 63cr; **Moulinsart:** 23tc; **Arne Naevra/Naturbilder:** 36r; **National Geographic Stock:** 19l, 23tr; Robert Campbell 60cl; Charles R. Knight 27bl; **naturepl.com:** Barrie Britton 101; Martin Dohrn 33tl; Pete Oxford 2bc, 18br, 36cl; Morley Read 20–21c; Anup Shah 40–41b; Jean-Pierre Zwaenepoel 35br; **New Zealand Post:** 22tl; **NHPA/Photoshot:** 40tl; Joe Blossom, 2tl, 32tl; Gerald Cubitt 65br; Jany Sauvanet 45br; **NOAA:** 18bl, 53cl; **PA Photos:** Doug Alft, 55tr; Hidajet Delic 26bl; Khalil Senosi 51tr; Photolibrary: Gerard Lacz 22b; OSF/Andrew Plumptre 61br; Oxford Scientific Films 47tc; **David Redfield/Research in Review Magazine, Florida State University:** 23bl; **Reuters:**

Ho New 61tl; **Francesco Rovero/Museo Tridentino di Scienze Naturali:** 19br; **Science Photo Library:** Georgette Douwma 37cl; Steve Gschmeissner 11c; Lawrence Lawry 20tl; Hank Morgan 57; Photo Researchers 55cr; Power and Syred 18c; Philippe Psaila 12t; Martin Shields 59tr; **The Telegraph Group:** 31cr; **University of Cambridge—University Library:** 10br; Ross Wanless/Percy FitzPatrck Institute of African Ornithology: 23tl; Fiona Watson/survivalinternational.org: 58bl; **Martin Williams:** 59tl

Wallchart: Alamy Images: Custom Life Science Images cl; **Ardea:** Kenneth W.Fink tr; **Corbis:** Bettmann cla, Tom Brakefield crb, Martin Harvey bl, Chris Hellier cra, Andrew Holbrooke cb; **Dorling Kindersley:** Frank Greenaway, Courtesy of the National Birds of Prey Center, Gloucestershire cla; **Getty Images:** Martin Harvey tl, Jeff Hunter c; **NHPA/Photoshot:** Joe Blossom cr; **PA Photos:** Doug Alft clb.

Jacket credits: Front: **Dorling Kindersley:** © David Peart (b); © Jerry Young (rhino). Back: NHPA/Photoshot: Thomas Arndt (tl). New Zealand Post Limited (tr). naturepl.com: Pete Oxford (cr). Alamy/Coinery (bc). Getty Images (br).

All other images © Dorling Kindersley
For further information see: www.dkimages.com

72